Introduction

More practice!

As the name suggests, this book is a volume of *more* Practice Exam Papers for Standard Grade General and Credit level English. Its sister publication (ISBN: 978-1-84372-768-2) Standard Grade General/Credit English Practice Papers for SQA Exams is also available and is packed full of entirely different practice exams A–C, worked solutions and helpful explanations, hints and exam tips.

More Standard Grade General/Credit English Practice Papers contains brand new practice exams, which mirror the actual SQA exam as closely as possible in question style, level, layout and appearance. It is a perfect way to familiarise yourself with the exam papers you will sit.

The answer section at the back of the book contains fully worked answers to each question, letting you know exactly where marks are gained in an answer and how the right answer is arrived at. It is also packed with explanatory notes and helpful advice to maximise your understanding of the types of questions you're likely to face in the exam.

How to use this book

The Practice Papers can be used in two main ways:

1. You can complete an entire practice paper as preparation for the final exam. If you would like to use the book in this way, you could complete the practice paper under exam-style conditions by setting yourself a time for each paper and answering it as well as possible without using any references or notes. Alternatively, you can answer the practice paper questions as a revision exercise, using your notes to produce a model answer. Your teacher may mark these for you.

2. You can use the Index of Question Types on page 6 to find out which types of questions are asked within each practice paper. You can also use this index to focus on a specific type of question which you would like to practise. For example, the index tells you which questions ask about punctuation. So you can practise answering specific questions about punctuation either at General or Credit level.

Revision advice

Work out a revision timetable for each week's work in advance – remember to cover all of your subjects and to leave time for homework and breaks. For example:

Day	6pm–6.45pm	7pm–8pm	8.15pm–9pm	9.15pm–10pm
Monday	Homework	Homework	**English revision**	Chemistry revision
Tuesday	Maths revision	Physics revision	Homework	Free
Wednesday	Geography revision	Modern Studies revision	**English revision**	French revision
Thursday	Homework	Maths revision	Chemistry revision	Free
Friday	Geography revision	French revision	Free	Free
Saturday	Free	Free	Free	Free
Sunday	Modern Studies revision	Maths revision	Modern Studies revision	Homework

Make sure that you have at least one evening free a week to relax, socialise and re-charge your batteries. It also gives your brain a chance to process the information that you have been feeding it all week.

Arrange your study time into one hour or 45 minute sessions, with a break between sessions, for example, 6pm–6.45pm, 7pm–7.45pm, 8.15pm–9pm. Try to start studying as early as possible in the evening when your brain is still alert and be aware that the longer you put off starting, the harder it will be to start!

Study a different subject in each session, except for the day before an exam.

Do something different during your breaks between study sessions – have a cup of tea, or listen to some music. Don't let your 15 minutes expand into 20 or 25 minutes though!

Have your class notes and any textbooks available for your revision to hand, as well as plenty of blank paper, a pen, etc. You may like to make keyword sheets like the geography example below.

Keyword	Meaning
Anticyclone	An area of high pressure
Secondary industry	Industry that manufactures things
Erosion	The process of wearing down the landscape

Finally, forget or ignore all or some of the advice in this section if you are happy with your present way of studying. Everyone revises differently, so find a way that works for you!

Transfer your knowledge

As well as using your class notes and textbooks to revise, these practice papers will also be a useful revision tool as they will help you to get used to answering exam-style questions. You may find as you work through the questions that they refer to a case-study or an example that you haven't come across before. Don't worry! You should be able to transfer your knowledge of a topic or theme to a new example. The enhanced answer section at the back will demonstrate how to read and interpret the question to identify the topic being examined and how to apply your course knowledge in order to answer the question successfully.

Command words

In the practice papers and in the exam itself, a number of command words will be used in the questions. These command words are used to show you how you should answer a question – some words indicate that you should write more than others. If you familiarise yourself with these command words, it will help you to structure your answers more effectively.

Command word(s)	Meaning/explanation
Analyse	Explain why a writer has written in a certain way.
Argue	State the arguments for or against a case.
Comment on	Explain and/or describe.
Compare	Give the key features of two different items or ideas and discuss their similarities and/or their differences.
Convey	Put across, communicate, tell.
Critically evaluate	Judge the success of a particular text.
Define	Give the meaning of.
Describe	Write in detail about the features of a movement/action/person/object.
Provide evidence	Find quotes from the passage.
Express	Write/explain.
Justify	Give reasons for your answer, stating why you have taken an action or reached a particular conclusion.
Suggest	Give an idea or suggestion.
Summarise	Condense into shortened form.

In the exam

The Reading examination takes 50 minutes. You should spend some of this time reading the passage. First, read through to get a general idea of what happens or what the passage is about. Then read through again. Perhaps this time, you could use a highlighter to highlight key words and phrases.

Now read the questions carefully. When you are ready to work through the questions, use the marks and the lines as a guide to how long your answer should be. There is more advice about this in the worked answers at the back of this book.

Always leave 5 minutes at the end to check your answers. Even if you have not finished the questions, try to take time for a check. This will ensure that your answers make sense and that they are spelt and punctuated correctly!

Watch your time and pace yourself carefully. Work out roughly how much time you can spend on each answer and try to stick to this.

Be clear before the exam what the instructions are likely to be, for example, how many questions you should answer in each section. The practice papers will help you to become familiar with the exam's instructions.

Read the question thoroughly before you begin to answer it – make sure you know exactly what the question is asking you to do. If the question is in sections, for example, 15a, 15b, 15c, make sure that you can answer each section before you start writing.

Give proper explanations. A common error is to give descriptions rather than explanations. If you are asked to explain something, you should be giving reasons. Check your answer and make sure that you have used plenty of linking words and phrases such as 'because', 'this means that', 'therefore', 'so', 'so that', 'due to', 'since' and 'the reason is'.

Good luck!

Index of Question Types

Topic	General Reading Exam D ('When sleep is just a dream')	Credit Reading Exam D ('Preferred Lies')	General Reading Exam E ('Never Let Me Go')	Credit Reading Exam E ('The God of Small Things')	General Reading Exam F ('The Kite Runner')	Credit Reading Exam F ('The Hungry Ghosts')	Knowledge for Prelim — Have difficulty	Knowledge for Prelim — Still needs work	Knowledge for Prelim — OK	Knowledge for SQA Exam — Have difficulty	Knowledge for SQA Exam — Still needs work	Knowledge for SQA Exam — OK
Understanding	3, 4, 7, 9, 12, 13, 16, 17	1, 3, 4, 5, 6, 7, 12, 13, 15, 17, 19, 20, 21	1, 2, 3, 5, 6, 8, 9, 10, 13, 14, 19, 20	1, 3, 7, 8, 9, 13, 14, 17	1, 3, 5, 7, 9, 11, 13, 14, 15, 16, 18, 20, 21	1, 2, 3, 6, 10, 12, 13, 14, 17, 19, 21, 22						
Evaluation	21, 22, 23	22, 23	23	22, 23	22	11, 23, 24						
Analysis – word choice	2, 10, 11, 19, 20, 24	2, 9, 14, 16	4, 16, 17, 18	2, 10, 11, 19, 20, 21	2	4, 5, 7, 8, 9, 16, 18, 20a, 20b						
Analysis – sentence structure		14, 18	11, 16	16		16						
Vocabulary	1, 5, 8(a/b)	8	7, 12, 15	4, 12	4, 6, 12							
Punctuation	6		21	6	8, 10							
Function	15	11	22	5, 18	17, 19	15						
Attitude	14, 18	10	24	15								

Understanding – questions which ask you about ideas or information in the passage.

Evaluation – questions which ask you for your opinion or judgement.

Analysis – questions which ask you about the writer's craft.

Vocabulary – questions which ask you about the meaning of a word(s).

Punctuation – questions which ask you about the use of punctuation.

Function – questions which ask you about the function of a word/sentence/paragraph.

Attitude – questions which ask you about the writer's attitude.

English   Standard Grade: General

Practice Papers
For SQA Exams

**General Level
Exam D
Reading**

Answer all of the questions.

Read the following passage and then answer the questions. Remember to use your own words as much as possible.

When sleep is just a dream

In this article from The Glasgow Herald, *the journalist Gordon Cairns describes a project which is designed to teach school pupils about the importance of sleep.*

1   Many a disengaged pupil has accused their teacher of putting them to sleep. But Glasgow teachers could soon be helping schoolchildren with advice on how to drop off.

2   In a unique project, Glasgow City Council is teaming up with a sleep counsellor to provide lessons for secondary pupils on how to avoid distractions and wind down. The council is concerned that increasingly pupils are unable to get the full nine hours sleep required to be able to learn, relax and be happy.

3   Under a new pilot scheme, four schools – Govan High, Bellahouston Academy, St Paul's Secondary and another school still to be determined – will bring sleep counsellor Nikki Cameron into the classroom to teach basic techniques.

4   Ms Cameron, who has worked extensively with the charity Sleep Scotland, says sleepless nights can have a major impact on academic performance. Research carried out by the University of Minnesota discovered A grade teenagers had on average 15 minutes', more sleep every night than those students mainly achieving Bs, who in turn averaged 11 minutes', more than those at level C.

5   'We can't be macho about sleep anymore, by seeing surviving on four hours a night as a virtue,' she said. 'Sleep is important for emotional and physical wellbeing and also for a young person learning, because that is when memories are processed, and the brain can store the learning.'

6   Jane Ansell is Sleep Scotland's director and has also helped thousands of children with disordered sleep patterns since her clinic was established 12 years ago. She said: 'Children need sleep to reach their full potential. You wouldn't send somebody to school without having the right amount of food, so why would you send them without enough sleep?'

7   More and more is known about the importance of a good night's sleep, Ms Ansell added: 'Sleep is when the brain rewires and consolidates the memory. If that is being deprived, not only do you have a kid who is too tired to concentrate, but also his brain won't work to full capacity.'

8   The flipside is that sleeping can be taught, if it is broken down into achievable steps and is positively enforced, she explains.

9   Ultimately, Sleep Scotland would like to see specialist teachers in every school in Scotland trained as sleep counsellors. The University of Dundee is already considering the introduction of a sleep counselling element in its teacher training programme.

10 Education expert Pamela Munn, retired Professor of Curriculum Research at Edinburgh University, recently co-authored a study into pupils' behaviour in Scottish schools. She believes lack of sleep is a contributing factor in the poor conduct of some pupils and supports attempts to timetable lessons in sleep.

11 She said: 'Our research has shown that quite a high percentage of pupil-to-pupil relationships, all over the school and in the classroom, have a degree of verbal and physical aggression. It is very plausible that sleep deprivation and poor diet can contribute to this.'

12 'When you are feeling tired, small things that you would normally have ignored start to irritate and upset you. Schools giving lessons about relaxation and sleeping would be very helpful in reducing the level of these incidents.'

13 As well as affecting behaviour and memory, lack of sleep may have other impacts. American research suggests teenagers who have fewer than five hours of sleep a night have a 71% higher risk of depression than those who slept eight hours.

14 Sleep Scotland also believes lack of sleep can cause misdiagnosis of conditions such as Attention Deficit Hyperactivity Disorder or at the very least make symptoms worse. The charity was created originally to help children with special needs with sleep problems and Ms Ansell says she has seen tired children misdiagnosed with conditions far more serious. She said: 'Teenagers who can't sleep sometimes get presented to us as either having Attention Deficit Hyperactivity Disorder or being on the autism spectrum. Until you solve the sleep problem you are not really sure what the underlying problem may be. The diagnosis can be reversible if they don't really have it.'

15 Pressures put on today's young adults are one factor causing sleeplessness, according to Cameron: 'This is a very stressed generation. They are under enormous pressure to do well in school, and there are far more things to do. Parents coming home from work will want to spend more time with their families which could all lead to them going to bed later than they should do, which is all going to have an effect.'

16 Bedrooms crammed with technological distractions are another bugbear. When Ansell is working with families, she tends to have the child's bedroom cleared of gadgets such as TVs and games consoles: 'Parents are making it more difficult for themselves and their kids through the use of this technology and the fact it has invaded the bedroom,' she says.

17 Some devices can affect levels of melatonin, a chemical which helps trigger drowsiness, in the body, she claims: 'Light coming from computers, TVs and mobile phones reduces the amount of melatonin in the body, which means you are making it harder for your body to close down. We all really need some separation between our living area and sleeping area to get a good night's rest.'

18 Ronnie Smith, General Secretary of the EIS, Scotland's largest teaching union, is not convinced that this is a generational issue.

19 Some pupils have always been sleep-deprived, but for different reasons, he suggests: 'Historically, children doing pre-school jobs like milk rounds would be coming to school tired but now we are getting reports of new distractions like TVs in the bedroom. For effective learning, the youngsters need to be alert; they need to be fed, watered and rested.'

20 Tony Waclawski, Glasgow City Council's Quality Improvement Officer Health Education (East), who welcomed Sleep Scotland into the classroom said: 'Sleep is an issue for young people in terms of them being fit to learn. Lack of sleep can cause them to be too tired to take information in properly in the classroom. We are committed to providing guidance to young people so they get the right amount of sleep and maximise their learning potential.'

Read paragraph 1 again.

		Marks

1. What does the word 'disengaged' suggest about some school pupils?

    _____

    _____

    2 ■ 0

2. What style of language is used in the expression 'drop off' and why has this been used?

    _____

    _____

    2 1 0

Read paragraphs 2 and 3 again.

3. Write down **two** pieces of evidence from paragraph 2 which tell you what pupils will learn about in sleep lessons.

    (i) _____

    (ii) _____

    2 1 0

4. **In your own words,** explain fully why the council is concerned about the problem of teenagers getting too little sleep.

    _____

    _____

    2 1 0

5. Write down **one** word from paragraph 2 which tells you that lessons in sleeping have not been taught before in Scotland and write down **one** phrase from paragraph 3 which continues this idea.

    Word [   ]

    Phrase _____

    2 1 0

6. What is the function of the dashes in paragraph 3?

    _____

    _____

    2 ■ 0

Read paragraph 4 again.

			Marks		

7. Complete the sentences below according to the University of Minnesota research described in paragraph 4. The first sentence has been completed for you.

Grade A teenagers get more sleep than students who achieve Grade B.

Grade B teenagers _____

Grade C teenagers _____   **2   1   0**

Read paragraph 5 again.

8. *(a)* What does the word 'macho' suggest about some young people's attitude to getting very little sleep?

_____

_____   **2   ■   0**

(b) What does the word 'virtue' suggest about some young people's attitude to getting very little sleep?

_____

_____   **2   ■   0**

9. According to Nikki Cameron, why is sleep important? Give **three** reasons.

(i) _____

(ii) _____

(iii) _____   **2   1   0**

Read paragraph 6 again.

10. Explain Jane Ansell's use of a question at the end of paragraph 6.

_____

_____   **2   ■   0**

Read paragraph 7 again.

11. In paragraph 5, Nikki Cameron is quoted as saying that sleep is important as 'that is when memories are processed and the brain can store learning'. Write down a phrase from paragraph 7 which continues this idea.

_____

_____

Read paragraph 8 again.

12. Jane Ansell suggests that sleeping can be taught in two ways. Explain these **in your own words**.

_____

_____

Read paragraphs 10, 11 and 12 again.

13. What is Professor Munn's attitude towards sleeping lessons in schools? Quote from the passage to support your answer.

_____

_____

14. **In your own words,** explain what Professor Munn's research shows about pupil-to-pupil relationships.

_____

_____

Read paragraphs 13 and 14 again.

15. What is the function of the sentence 'As well as affecting behaviour and memory, lack of sleep may have other impacts.'?

_____

_____

	Marks	
2	■	0
2	1	0
2	1	0
2	1	0
2	1	0

16. It is stated that lack of sleep may have 'other impacts'.
Explain what these other impacts might be.

_____

_____

2 | 1 | 0

Read paragraphs 15 and 16 again.

17. In your own words, explain what two things parents could do to improve the sleeping habits of their children.

_____

_____

2 | 1 | 0

18. What is Jane Ansell's attitude towards technology in teenagers' bedrooms? Quote a word or phrase from paragraph 16 to support your answer.

_____

_____

2 | 1 | 0

Read paragraph 19 again.

19. In paragraph 19, Ronnie Smith states that youngsters 'need to be fed, watered and rested.' Comment fully on the speaker's word choice.

_____

_____

2 | 1 | 0

Read paragraph 20 again.

20. Tony Waclawski wants young people to 'maximise their learning potential'. Explain what this phrase means **in your own words**.

_____

_____

2 | ■ | 0

Marks

Now think about the passage as a whole.

	Marks

21. The title of this article is 'When sleep is just a dream'. Do you think this is an effective title? Give a reason for your answer.

_____

_____

_____   2   1   0

22. In your opinion, who is most likely to read this article? Give a reason for your answer.

_____

_____

_____   2   1   0

23. What is the writer's main purpose in writing this article? Tick **one** box only and explain the reason for your choice.

To inform the reader about the importance of sleep.	
To argue against giving school pupils sleeping lessons.	
To argue for giving school pupils sleeping lessons.	

_____

_____   2   1   0

24. Identify and comment on any technique which the writer uses to add weight to the information in the article.

_____

_____

_____   2   1   0

English　　　　Standard Grade: Credit

Practice Papers　　　　　　　　　　　　　　　　　　**Credit Level**
For SQA Exams　　　　　　　　　　　　　　　　　　**Exam D**
　　　　　　　　　　　　　　　　　　　　　　　　　　　Reading

Answer all of the questions.

Read the following passage and then answer the questions. Remember to use your own words as much as possible.

Scotland's leading educational publishers

Preferred Lies

In this extract from his book Preferred Lies, *Andrew Greig, a well-known Scottish writer, describes his first day at boarding school.*

1   I'd been eleven when my parents left me at boarding school. I see crowds of bigger boys charging round shouting. My father gives me a manly handshake, my mother a brief hug. I'll see them in a couple of months. Then they're gone and I'm sitting amid the din in my brand-new uniform on my trunk with my name stencilled on it, containing my new clothes for the year, each item with my name tag sewn onto it, down to the last sock and handkerchief. It might as well be a number.

2   I've left behind my parents, the dog, my wee brother, my games, the books, toys, clothes, freedoms of my former life. My big brother and sister are here, but in other boarding houses, and our paths won't cross often. I'm on my own in this bewildering world and I have to survive it. My only luxury and friend is across my knee; a pencil bag containing half a dozen clubs, a few tees and some found balls. This golf bag has no name tag on it, but at least it is mine.

3   Presumably, everyone has a period in their lives they can identify as simply wretched, and those two years at boarding school were mine. Perhaps if I'd stayed on through the school, like my elder brother and sister, I'd have been more positive about it.

4   But I came in near the bottom and left near the bottom, and it was rotten. Something to be endured at best. I'd run away twice. I had absolutely no memory of this, but it seemed like a very good idea. When my dad retired and moved, he accepted it when I said I wanted to go to the local school. It couldn't possibly be any worse.

5   Most of the time, I don't even think of boarding school. The Former Pupil newsletter goes straight in the bin. And yet the memory surfaces once in a while, the pain and anger still as freshly cut as the day they were stamped.

6   Maybe it's time to finally accept, and outgrow, the things learned back then. We are so malleable, so porous in childhood. We're surprisingly tough, yet we mark easily.

7   When people talk, as they do in all sincerity, about the team spirit, self-reliance and self-confidence that can come from boarding school, I see the games room after the evening meal on that first day.

8   All us new boys were herded in by the head of the house and his cohorts (who I now see were only fifteen-year-old knobbly-kneed pimply youths but then were

powerful, irresistible figures). The house master and matron had disappeared. The door was shut, the table tennis table moved aside. There was an uneasy silence. Some heavy leather footballs were brought out. We were commanded to line up against the far wall, facing out.

9   'Right! The rules are you mustn't turn away or put your hands up to protect your face. Got that? Anyone who does will be beaten!'

10   Who were you, red-faced shouting boy terrorizing children in the name of tradition, what had they done to you? What did you go on to do? Did you become a bully in the army, or law, or a god-like consultant in medicine? Perhaps you became a director in the family firm, your wife detests you, your children went to boarding school and became strangers to you. Or maybe, just maybe, you grew up and became a decent, useful human being, kind to friends, decent to strangers, loyal and close to your loving wife and children. Perhaps we passed in the street last week.

11   Whoever or wherever, the boy in me still loathes you.

12   So we were lined up against the wall at one end of the games room, the head of house and his prefects with the footballs at the other end 25 feet away. Whatever was coming, it wasn't going to be good.

13   'Wait!'

14   One of the prefects walked up, looked at me impassively, almost sympathetically, then carefully removed my glasses, put them in his pocket.

15   'You'll get these back later.'

16   Then they began kicking the heavy footballs at us as hard as possible. No turning away, no putting up hands. Mayhem of thudding, shouting, battering, crying. A ball hit me full on the face and I felt unreal after that, passive, went deep inside myself to outlast it. I sometimes wonder how long I stayed like that.

17   This initiation lasted maybe twenty minutes. Physical results; a few bloody noses, bruises, shocks and tears. No lasting physical damage of course but enough to break us in. To make it clear we no longer had any individual dignity, freedom, value. Here we would do what we were told because we were told, and take what was coming to us and not ask why.

18   Then it was over. The footballs bounced and were silent. A few boys were whimpering, one cried loudly. I was still far away, lying by the river at the bottom of our garden.

19 'SHUT UP!'

20 I was handed back my glasses. Whenever I read about torture chambers, beaten confessions, punishment beatings, it is that gloomy green-painted games room that I see. And it is one of the many terrible things in our world that makes me angry rather than sad: the power of the strong over the weak. Or put it simply: bullying.

Read paragraph 1 again.

	Marks	

1. What is the writer's first impression of his boarding school?
    Quote to support your answer.

    _____

    _____   **2 1 0**

2. Why does the writer use the present tense when describing his first day at boarding school?

    _____

    _____   **2 ■ 0**

3. **In your own words,** explain what the writer means by 'It might as well be a number.'

    _____

    _____   **2 ■ 0**

Read paragraph 2 again.

4. **In your own words,** explain fully what the writer has left behind.

    _____

    _____   **2 1 0**

5. Why will the writer not see his big brother and sister very often?
    Quote from the passage to support your answer.

    _____

    _____   **2 1 0**

6. What is the writer's only 'luxury and friend' and why does he feel this way about it?

    _____

    _____   **2 1 0**

Marks

Read paragraph 3 again.

7. (*a*) What period in his life does the writer think was 'wretched'?

    _____ | 2 | ■ | 0 |

    (*b*) Does the writer think everyone has a 'wretched' period in their lives? Quote from the passage to support your answer.

    _____ | 2 | 1 | 0 |

Read paragraph 4 again.

8. Give the meaning of 'endured' and show how the context helped you to arrive at the meaning.

    _____

    _____ | 2 | 1 | 0 |

Read paragraph 5 again.

9. Identify the image the writer uses in the phrase 'And yet the memory surfaces once in a while' and comment on its effectiveness.

    _____

    _____

    _____ | 2 | 1 | 0 |

Read paragraph 7 again.

10. What is the writer's attitude to people who talk about the positive aspects of boarding school? Quote to support your answer.

    _____

    _____ | 2 | 1 | 0 |

11. What is the function of the phrase 'I see the games room after the evening meal on that first day'?

    _____

    _____ | 2 | 1 | 0 |

	Marks	

Read paragraph 8 again.

12. What did the writer think about the older boys **then** and how does he feel about them **now**?

_____

_____

2 1 0

13. In your opinion, why was there an 'uneasy silence'? Quote to support your answer.

_____

_____

2 1 0

Read paragraph 10 again.

14. Identify one technique the writer uses in this paragraph to show how he feels about the head of house and explain how it does so.

_____

_____

2 1 0

15. The writer gives two contrasting descriptions of the bully as an adult. Referring to the paragraph as a whole, explain these **in your own words**.

_____

_____

2 1 0

Read paragraphs 13, 14 and 15 again.

16. Identify **one** way in which the writer creates tension in this section and explain how it does so.

_____

_____

2 1 0

Read paragraph 16 again.

17. **In your own words**, explain what happened to the new boys in the games room and how the new boys reacted to this.

_____

_____

2 1 0

18. 'Mayhem of thudding, shouting, battering, crying.'
Comment on the effectiveness of the sentence structure used here.

_____

_____

2 | 1 | 0

19. (a) Explain **in your own words** how the writer copes with the pain of being hit.

_____

_____

2 | ■ | 0

(b) Write down a sentence from paragraph 18 which continues this idea.

_____

_____

2 | ■ | 0

Read paragraph 17 again.

20. To what extent were the boys physically injured during the incident?
Give evidence from the passage to support your answer.

_____

_____

2 | 1 | 0

21. In the writer's opinion, what was the purpose of the initiation?

_____

_____

2 | ■ | 0

Read paragraph 19 again.

22. 'SHUT UP!' In your opinion, who shouts this and why?

_____

_____

2 | 1 | 0

Think about the passage as a whole.

23. In your opinion, what is the writer's purpose in writing this passage?
    Give evidence from the passage to support your answer.

    _____

    _____

    _____

Marks		
2	1	0

English Standard Grade: General

Practice Papers
For SQA Exams

General Level
Exam E
Reading

Answer all of the questions.

Read the following passage and then answer the questions. Remember to use your own words as much as possible.

Never Let Me Go

In the novel Never Let Me Go *by Kazuo Ishiguro, Kathy, one of the main characters, remembers an incident at boarding school.*

1   On the particular afternoon I'm now thinking of, we were standing up on stools and benches, crowding around the high windows. That gave us a clear view of the North Playing Field where about a dozen boys from our year and Senior 3 had gathered to play football. There was bright sunshine, but it must have been raining earlier that day because I can remember how the sun was glinting on the muddy surface of the grass.

2   Someone said we shouldn't be so obvious about watching, but we hardly moved back at all. Then Ruth said: 'He doesn't suspect a thing. Look at him. He really doesn't suspect a thing.'

3   When she said this, I looked at her and searched for signs of disapproval about what the boys were going to do to Tommy. But the next second Ruth gave a little laugh and said: 'The idiot!'

4   And I realised that for Ruth and the others, whatever the boys chose to do was pretty remote from us; whether we approved or not didn't come into it. We were gathered around the windows at that moment not because we relished the prospect of seeing Tommy get humiliated yet again, but just because we'd heard about this latest plot and were vaguely curious to watch it unfold. In those days, I don't think what the boys did amongst themselves went much deeper than that. For Ruth, for the others, it was that detached, and the chances are that's how it was for me too.

5   Or maybe I'm remembering it wrong. Maybe even then, when I saw Tommy rushing about that field, undisguised delight on his face to be accepted back in the fold again, about to play the game at which he so excelled, maybe I did feel a little stab of pain. What I do remember is that I noticed Tommy was wearing the light blue polo shirt he'd got in the sales the previous month – the one he was so proud of. I remember thinking: 'He's really stupid, playing football in that. It'll get ruined, then how's he going to feel?' Out loud, I said, to no one in particular: 'Tommy's got his shirt on. His favourite polo shirt.'

6   I don't think anyone heard me, because they were all laughing at Laura – the big clown in our group – mimicking one after the other the expressions that appeared on Tommy's face as he ran, waved, called, tackled. The other boys were all moving around the field in that deliberately languorous way they have when they're warming up, but Tommy, in his excitement, seemed already to be going full pelt. I said, louder this time: 'He's going to be so sick if he ruins that shirt.' This time Ruth heard me, but she must have thought I'd meant it as some kind of joke, because she laughed half-heartedly, then made some quip of her own.

7   Then the boys had stopped kicking the ball about, and were standing in a pack in the mud, their chests gently rising and falling as they waited for the team picking to start. The two captains who emerged were from Senior 3, though everyone knew Tommy was a better player than any of that year. They tossed for first pick, then the one who'd won stared at the group.

8   'Look at him,' someone behind me said. 'He's completely convinced he's going to be first pick. Just look at him!'

9   There was something comical about Tommy at that moment, something that made you think, well, yes, if he's going to be that daft, he deserves what's coming. The other boys were all pretending to ignore the picking process, pretending they didn't care where they came in the order. Some were talking quietly to each other, some re-tying their laces, others just staring down at their feet as they trammelled the mud. But Tommy was looking eagerly at the Senior 3 boy, as though his name had already been called.

10   Laura kept up her performance all through the team-picking, doing all the different expressions that went across Tommy's face: the bright eager one at the start; the puzzled concern when four picks had gone by and he still hadn't been chosen; the hurt and panic as it began to dawn on him what was really going on. I didn't keep glancing round at Laura, though, because I was watching Tommy; I only knew what she was doing because the others kept laughing and egging her on. Then when Tommy was left standing alone, and the boys all began sniggering, I heard Ruth say:

11   'It's coming. Hold it. Seven seconds. Seven, six, five . . .'

12   She never got there. Tommy burst into thunderous bellowing, and the boys, now laughing openly, started to run off towards the South Playing Field. Tommy took a few strides after them – it was hard to say whether his instinct was to give angry chase or if he was panicked at being left behind. In any case he soon stopped and stood there, glaring after them, his face scarlet. Then he began to scream and shout, a nonsensical jumble of swear words and insults.

13   We'd all seen plenty of Tommy's tantrums by then, so we came down off our stools and spread ourselves around the room. We tried to start up a conversation about something else, but there was Tommy going on and on in the background, and although at first we just rolled our eyes and tried to ignore it, in the end – probably a full ten minutes after we'd first moved away – we were back up at the windows again.

14   'I suppose it is a bit cruel,' Ruth said, 'the way they always work him up like that. But it's his own fault. If he learnt to keep his cool, they'd leave him alone.'

		Marks

Read paragraph 1 again.

1. Why were Kathy and Ruth standing on stools and benches?

    _____

    _____   2   1   0

2. **In your own words,** explain why Kathy thinks it must have been raining earlier in the day.

    _____

    _____   2   1   0

Read paragraph 2 again.

3. **In your own words,** explain why someone suggests that Kathy and Ruth should move back from the windows.

    _____

    _____   2   ■   0

4. Comment on the effect of the writer's word choice in 'He doesn't suspect a thing. Look at him. He really doesn't suspect a thing.'

    _____

    _____   2   1   0

Read paragraph 3 again.

5. Write down three pieces of evidence which show that Ruth approves of what is about to happen.

    (i) _____

    (ii) _____

    (iii) _____   2   1   0

		Marks	

Read paragraph 4 again.

6. What reasons does Kathy give for watching Tommy and the football game? Tick the reasons which are true in the box below.

The girls knew something had been planned.	
The girls were slightly interested in what was going to happen at the football match.	
The girls were looking forward to seeing Tommy's embarrassment.	

2 1 0

7. '[W]hatever the boys chose to do was pretty remote from us;'. Write down a word from later in the paragraph which is similar in meaning to 'remote'.

[   ]

2 ■ 0

Read paragraph 5 again.

8. Write down two pieces of evidence from the passage which show that Tommy was enjoying the game of football.

   (i) _____

   (ii) _____

2 1 0

9. **In your own words,** explain why Kathy is concerned about Tommy's shirt.

   _____

   _____

2 1 0

Read paragraph 6 again.

10. What was Laura doing while Tommy was playing? Answer **in your own words**.

   _____

   _____

2 1 0

11. Comment on the effectiveness of the writer's structure in the phrase 'as he ran, waved, called, tackled'.

   _____

   _____

2 1 0

12. Give the meaning of 'quip' and show how the context helped you to arrive at the meaning.

_____

_____

Read paragraph 9 again.

13. The boys react differently to the 'picking process' when the team captains choose their team players. How do the boys react and how does Tommy react?

(*a*) The other boys: _____

_____

(*b*) Tommy: _____

_____

Read paragraph 10 again.

14. What three different expressions showed on Tommy's face? **Use your own words** in your answer.

(i) _____

(ii) _____

(iii) _____

15. Tick the phrase which is closest in meaning to 'egging her on'.

Throwing eggs at her	
Encouraging her	
Sniggering at her	
Pushing her to the front	

Read paragraph 11 again.

16. 'It's coming. Hold it. Seven seconds. Seven, six, five . . .' By referring to word choice or sentence structure, show how the writer creates tension in these lines.

_____

_____

Marks		
2	1	0
2	1	0
2	1	0
2	1	0
2	■	0
2	1	0

		Marks

Read paragraph 12 again.

17. How effective do you find the writer's word choice in the phrase 'thunderous bellowing'?

_____

_____

2 ■ 0

18. By referring closely to the passage, explain how the writer's word choice indicates the intensity of Tommy's feelings after the boys have run off.

_____

_____

2 1 0

Read paragraph 13 again.

19. In your opinion, why did the children come back down from the windows? Use evidence from the passage to support your answer.

_____

_____

2 1 0

20. Why are dashes used in the sentence '. . . in the end – probably a full ten minutes after we'd first moved away – we were back up at the windows again.'

_____

_____

2 ■ 0

Read paragraph 14 again.

21. How effective is this paragraph as a conclusion to the passage? Give evidence from the passage to support your answer.

_____

_____

_____

2 1 0

Think about the passage as a whole.

	Marks	

22. In your opinion, what are Kathy's feelings towards Tommy? Give evidence from the passage to support your answer.

_____

_____

_____

| 2 | 1 | 0 |

23. Explain fully whether you think Kathy's memories are **accurate.** Quote from the passage to support your answer.

_____

_____

_____

| 2 | 1 | 0 |

24. In your opinion, what is the writer's attitude towards boarding schools? Give a reason for your answer.

_____

_____

_____

| 2 | 1 | 0 |

Exam E – Credit Paper

English   Standard Grade: Credit

Practice Papers
For SQA Exams

Credit Level
Exam E
Reading

Answer all of the questions.

Read the following passage and then answer the questions. Remember to use your own words as much as possible.

The God of Small Things

In this extract from Arundhati Roy's novel The God of Small Things, *the writer describes Estha, who is separated from his twin sister Rahel after the death of his cousin Sophie Mol.*

1   Estha had always been a quiet child, so no one could pinpoint with any degree of accuracy exactly when (the year, if not the month or day) he had stopped talking. Stopped talking altogether, that is. The fact is that there wasn't an 'exactly when'. It had been a gradual winding down and closing shop. A barely noticeable quietening. As though he had simply run out of conversation and had nothing left to say. Yet Estha's silence was never awkward. Never intrusive. Never noisy.

2   Over time he had acquired the ability to blend into the background of wherever he was – into bookshelves, gardens, curtains, doorways, streets – to appear inanimate, almost invisible to the untrained eye. It usually took strangers a while to notice him even when they were in the same room with him. It took them even longer to notice that he never spoke. Some never noticed at all.

3   Estha occupied very little space in the world.

4   After Sophie Mol's funeral, when Estha was Returned, their father sent him to a boys' school in Calcutta. He was not an exceptional student, but neither was he backward, nor particularly bad at anything. An average student, or Satisfactory work were the usual comments that his teachers wrote in his Annual Progress Reports. Does not participate in Group Activities was another recurring complaint. Though what exactly they meant by 'Group Activities' they never said.

5   Estha finished school with mediocre results, but refused to go to college. Instead, much to the initial embarrassment of his father and stepmother, he began to do the housework. As though in his own way he was trying to earn his keep. He did the sweeping, swabbing and all the laundry. He learned to cook and shop for vegetables. Vendors in the bazaar, sitting behind pyramids of oiled, shining vegetables, grew to recognize him and would attend to him amidst the clamoring of their other customers. They gave him rusted film cans in which to put the vegetables he picked. He never bargained. They never cheated him. When the vegetables had been weighed and paid for, they would transfer them to his red plastic shopping basket (onions at the bottom, aubergines and tomatoes on the top) and always a sprig of coriander and a fistful of green chilies for free. Estha carried them home in the crowded tram. A quiet bubble floating on a sea of noise.

6   At mealtimes, when he wanted something, he got up and helped himself.

7   Once the quietness arrived, it stayed and spread in Estha. It reached out of his head and enfolded him in its swampy arms. It rocked him to the rhythm of an ancient, fetal heartbeat. It sent its stealthy, suckered tentacles inching along the insides of his skull, hoovering the knolls and dells of his memory, dislodging old sentences, whisking them off the tip of his tongue. It stripped his thoughts of the words that described them and left them pared and naked. Unspeakable. Numb. And to an observer therefore, perhaps barely there.

8   Slowly, over the years, Estha withdrew from the world. He grew accustomed to the uneasy octopus that lived inside him and squirted its inky tranquilizer on his past. Gradually the reason for his silence was hidden away, entombed somewhere deep in the soothing folds of the fact of it.

9   When Khubchand, his beloved, blind, bald, incontinent seventeen-year-old mongrel decided to stage a miserable, long-drawn-out death, Estha started his walking. He walked for hours on end. Initially he patrolled only the neighborhood, but gradually went farther and farther afield.

10 People got used to seeing him on the road. A well-dressed man with a quiet walk. His face grew dark and outdoorsy. Rugged. Wrinkled by the sun. He began to look wiser than he really was. Like a fisherman in a city. With sea-secrets in him.

11 Some days he walked along the banks of the river that smelled of shit and pesticides bought with World Bank loans. Most of the fish had died. The ones that survived suffered from fin-rot and had broken out in boils.

12 Other days he walked down the road. Past the new, freshly baked, iced, Gulf-money houses built by nurses, masons, wire-benders and bank clerks, who worked hard and unhappily in faraway places. Past the resentful older houses tinged green with envy, cowering in their private driveways among their private rubber trees.

13 He walked past the village school that his great-grandfather built for Untouchable children. Past Sophie Mol's yellow church. Past the Ayemenem Youth Kung Fu Club. Past the Tender Buds Nursery School (for Touchables), past the ration shop that sold rice, sugar and bananas that hung in yellow bunches from the roof.

14 It had been quiet in Estha's head until Rahel came. But with her she had brought the sound of passing trains, and the light and shade and light and shade that falls on you if you have a window seat. The world, locked out for years, suddenly flooded in, and now Estha couldn't hear himself for the noise. Trains. Traffic. Music. The stock market. A dam had burst and savage waters swept everything up in a swirling. Comets, violins, parades, loneliness, clouds, beards, bigots, lists, flags, earthquakes, despair were all swept up in a scrambled swirling.

15   And Estha, walking on the riverbank, couldn't feel the wetness of the rain, or the suddenshudder of the cold puppy that had temporarily adopted him and squelched at his side. He walked past the old mango tree and up to the edge of a clay spur that jutted out into the river. He squatted on his haunches and rocked himself in the rain. The wet mud under his shoes made rude, sucking sounds. The cold puppy shivered and watched.

	Marks		

Read paragraph 1 again.

1. Why did no one know the exact date when Estha stopped talking?
    Quote to support your answer.

    _____

    _____ | 2 | 1 | 0 |

2. 'Yet Estha's silence was never awkward. Never intrusive. Never noisy.' Explain fully how the writer's **word choice** in these lines indicates what Estha's silence was like.

    _____

    _____ | 2 | 1 | 0 |

Read paragraph 2 again.

3. What is the meaning of 'inanimate' and how does the context help you to work out the meaning? Give a reason for your answer.

    _____

    _____ | 2 | 1 | 0 |

4. How did strangers react to Estha's silence?

    _____

    _____ | 2 | 1 | 0 |

Read paragraph 3 again.

5. What is the function of the sentence 'Estha occupied very little space in the world.'?

    _____

    _____ | 2 | ■ | 0 |

Marks

Read paragraph 4 again.

6. Suggest why a capital letter is used at the beginning of 'Returned'.

_____

_____

2 ■ 0

7. **In your own words,** what type of student was Estha?

_____

_____

2 1 0

Read paragraph 5 again.

8. **In your own words,** explain fully how Estha's parents felt about Estha doing housework.

_____

_____

2 1 0

9. **In your own words,** give two reasons why the vendors in the bazaar were kind to Estha.

_____

_____

2 1 0

10. (*a*) Comment fully on the effectiveness of the image 'A quiet bubble floating on a sea of noise.'

_____

_____

2 1 0

(*b*) Write down an image from paragraph 14 which extends this idea.

_____

_____

2 1 0

Read paragraph 7 again.

11. Identify any **two** techniques used by the writer which help to convey how quietness spread through Estha. Quote from the passage to support your answers.

Technique 1: _____

_____

2 | 1 | 0

Technique 2: _____

_____

2 | 1 | 0

Read paragraph 8 again.

12. What is the meaning of 'entombed' and how does the context help you to work out the meaning? Give a reason for your answer.

_____

_____

2 | 1 | 0

Read paragraph 9 again.

13. In your own words, explain how Estha's walking changed.

_____

_____

2 | 1 | 0

Read paragraph 10 again.

14. Write down **two** pieces of evidence from the passage which show that Estha 'began to look wiser than he really was'.

(i) _____

(ii) _____

2 | 1 | 0

Marks

Read paragraph 11 again.

15. What is the writer's attitude towards loans from the World Bank?
Write down a piece of evidence from the passage to support your answer.

_____

_____

2 1 0

Read paragraph 12 again.

16. The writer contrasts the new houses and the old houses which Estha passes while walking. **In your own words,** state what the contrast is.

_____

_____

2 1 0

Read paragraph 14 again.

17. Comment on the effectiveness of the structure 'Comets, violins, parades, loneliness, clouds, beards, bigots, lists, flags, earthquakes, despair'.

_____

_____

2 1 0

18. How does the first sentence of paragraph 14 act as a link between the previous paragraphs and the paragraphs which follow?

_____

_____

2 1 0

19. 'But with her she had brought the sound of passing trains, and the light and shade and light and shade that falls on you if you have a window seat.'

Comment fully on the effectiveness of the writer's word choice in this sentence.

_____

_____

2 1 0

	Marks	

Read paragraph 15 again.

20. Estha's puppy 'squelched at his side'. Comment fully on the writer's word choice and whether you find it effective.

_____

_____

| 2 | 1 | 0 |

21. What mood or atmosphere does the writer create in the last paragraph? Give evidence from the paragraph to support your answer.

_____

_____

_____

| 2 | 1 | 0 |

Think about the passage as a whole.

22. In your opinion, does Estha change in the course of the passage?

_____

_____

_____

| 2 | 1 | 0 |

23. Do you feel sympathy for the character of Estha? Give reasons for your answer by referring closely to the passage.

_____

_____

| 2 | 1 | 0 |

Exam F – General Paper

English   Standard Grade: General

Practice Papers
For SQA Exams

**General Level
Exam F
Reading**

Answer all of the questions.

Read the following passage and then answer the questions. Remember to use your own words as much as possible.

The Kite Runner

In this extract from the novel The Kite Runner *by Khaled Hosseini, the narrator describes memories of his childhood friendship with Hassan in Afghanistan.*

1   When we were children, Hassan and I used to climb the poplar trees in the driveway of my father's house and annoy the neighbors by reflecting sunlight into their homes with a shard of mirror. We would sit across from each other on a pair of high branches, our naked feet dangling, our trouser pockets filled with dried mulberries and walnuts. We took turns with the mirror as we ate the mulberries, pelted each other with them, giggling, laughing. I can still see Hassan up on that tree, sunlight flickering through the leaves on his almost perfectly round face, a face like a Chinese doll chiseled from hardwood: his flat, broad nose and slanting, narrow eyes like bamboo leaves, eyes that looked, depending on the light, gold, green, even sapphire. I can still see his tiny low-set ears and that pointed stub of a chin, a meaty piece of skin that looked like it was added as a mere afterthought. And the split lip, just left of mid-line, where the Chinese doll maker's instrument may have slipped, or perhaps he had simply grown tired and careless.

2   Sometimes, up in those trees, I talked Hassan into firing walnuts with his slingshot at the neighbor's one-eyed dog. Hassan never wanted to, but if I asked, really asked, he wouldn't deny me. Hassan never denied me anything. And he was deadly with his slingshot. Hassan's father, Ali, used to catch us and get mad, or as mad as someone as gentle as Ali could ever get. He would wag his finger and wave us down from the tree. He would take the mirror and tell us what his mother had told him, that the devil shone mirrors too, shone them to distract Muslims during prayer. 'And he laughs while he does it,' he always added, scowling at his son. 'Yes, Father,' Hassan would mumble, looking down at his feet. But he never told on me. Never told that the mirror, like shooting walnuts at the neighbor's dog, was always my idea.

3   The poplar trees lined the redbrick driveway, which led to a pair of wrought-iron gates. They in turn opened to an extension of the driveway into my father's estate. The house sat on the left side of the brick path, the backyard at the end of it. Everyone agreed that my father, my Baba, had built the most beautiful house in the Wazir Akbar Khan district, a new and affluent neighborhood in the northern part of Kabul. Some thought it was the prettiest house in all of Kabul. A broad entryway flanked by rosebushes led to the sprawling house of marble floors and wide windows. Intricate mosaic tiles, handpicked by Baba in Isfahan, covered the floors of the four bathrooms. Gold-stitched tapestries, which Baba had bought in Calcutta, lined the walls; a crystal chandelier hung from the vaulted ceiling.

4   Upstairs was my bedroom, Baba's room, and his study, also known as 'the smoking room,' which perpetually smelled of tobacco and cinnamon. Baba and his friends reclined on black leather chairs there after Ali had served dinner. They stuffed their pipes – except Baba always called it 'fattening the pipe' – and discussed their favorite three topics: politics, business, soccer. Sometimes I asked Baba if I could sit with them, but Baba would stand in the doorway. 'Go on, now,' he'd say. 'This is grown-ups' time. Why don't you go and read one of those books of yours?' He'd close the door, leave me to wonder why it was always grown-ups' time with him. I'd sit by the door, knees drawn to my chest. Sometimes I sat there for an hour, sometimes two, listening to their laughter, their chatter.

5   The living room downstairs had a curved wall with custom-built cabinets. Inside sat framed family pictures: an old, grainy photo of my grandfather and King Nadir Shah taken in 1931, two years before the king's assassination; they are standing over a dead deer, dressed in knee high boots, rifles slung over their shoulders. There was a picture of my parents' wedding night, Baba dashing in his black suit and my mother a smiling young princess in white. Here was Baba and his best friend and business partner, Rahim Khan, standing outside our house, neither one smiling – I am a baby in that photograph and Baba is holding me, looking tired and grim. I'm in his arms, but it's Rahim Khan's pinky my fingers are curled around.

6   The curved wall led into the dining room, at the center of which was a mahogany table that could easily sit thirty guests – and, given my father's taste for extravagant parties, it did just that almost every week. On the other end of the dining room was a tall marble fireplace, always lit by the orange glow of a fire in the wintertime. A large sliding glass door opened into the semicircular terrace that overlooked two acres of backyard and rows of cherry trees. Baba and Ali had planted a small vegetable garden along the eastern wall: tomatoes, mint, peppers and a row of corn that never really took. Hassan and I used to call it 'the Wall of Ailing Corn'. On the south end of the garden, in the shadows of the fruit tree, was the servants' home, a modest little mud hut where Hassan lived with his father.

7   It was there, in that little shack, that Hassan was born in the winter of 1964, just one year after my mother died giving birth to me.

8   In the eighteen years that I lived in that house, I stepped into Hassan and Ali's quarters only a handful of times. When the sun dropped low behind the hills and we were done playing for the day, Hassan and I parted ways. I went past the rosebushes to Baba's mansion, Hassan to the mud shack where he had been born, where he'd lived his entire life.

9   It was in that small shack that Hassan's mother, Sanaubar, gave birth to him one cold winter day in 1964. While my mother hemorrhaged to death during childbirth, Hassan lost his less than a week after he was born. Lost her to a fate most Afghans considered far worse than death: she ran off with a clan of travelling singers and dancers.

Read paragraph 1 again.

		Marks

1. How did Hassan and the narrator annoy the neighbours?
    Answer fully **in your own words**.

    _____

    _____

    | 2 | 1 | 0 |

2. Write down a simile from paragraph 1 and comment on its effectiveness.

    _____

    _____

    | 2 | 1 | 0 |

Read paragraph 2 again.

3. 'Hassan never denied me anything.' Explain what this phrase means **in your own words**.

    _____

    _____

    | 2 | ■ | 0 |

4. Write down a word from paragraph 2 which shows that Hassan was good at using the slingshot.

    ```
    [                    ]
    ```

    | 2 | ■ | 0 |

5. How angry was Ali, Hassan's father, with the boys? Find evidence from the passage to support your answer.

    _____

    _____

    | 2 | 1 | 0 |

Read paragraph 3 again.

6. The narrator's house is in an 'affluent' neighbourhood. Tick the word below which is nearest in meaning to 'affluent'.

well-off	
crowded	
polluted	
large	

    | 2 | ■ | 0 |

		Marks	

7. Write down two reasons from the section after this phrase which explain why people might think the narrator's house was 'the prettiest house in all of Kabul'.

(i) _____

(ii) _____   **2 1 0**

Read paragraph 4 again.

8. Suggest why quotation marks are used around the phrase 'the smoking room'.

_____

_____   **2 ■ 0**

9. What do Baba and his friends do in 'the smoking room' after dinner? Answer **in your own words**.

_____

_____   **2 1 0**

10. (*a*) Why are dashes used in the sentence 'They stuffed their pipes – except Baba always called it "fattening the pipe" – and discussed their favorite three topics: politics, business, soccer.'?

_____

_____   **2 ■ 0**

(*b*) Write down another example of dashes used for the same reason from later in the passage.

_____   **■ 1 0**

11. In your opinion, does Baba spend a lot of time with his son? Quote from the passage to support your answer.

_____

_____   **2 1 0**

Read paragraph 5 again.

12. What does the phrase 'custom-built cabinets' mean?
Show how the context helped you to arrive at the meaning.

_____

_____

| | 2 | 1 | 0 |

13. The narrator describes three framed photographs. Write down the people shown in each photograph.

(i) _____

(ii) _____

(iii) _____

| 3 | 2 | 1 | 0 |

14. In your opinion, which is the best photograph? Quote from the passage to support your answer.

_____

_____

| | 2 | 1 | 0 |

Read paragraph 6 again.

15. (a) Explain **in your own words** why Baba's parties are 'extravagant'.

_____

_____

| | 2 | 1 | 0 |

(b) Write down one word from later in the paragraph which means the **opposite** of 'extravagant'.

| | 2 | ■ | 0 |

16. Why was 'the Wall of Ailing Corn' an appropriate name for the row of corn?

_____

_____

| | 2 | 1 | 0 |

Read paragraph 7 again.

17. Comment on why you think paragraph 7 has been placed on its own.

_____

_____

| 2 | 1 | 0 |

Read paragraph 8 again.

18. In your opinion, why did the narrator visit Hassan and Ali's quarters 'only a handful of times' in 18 years?

_____

_____

| 2 | ■ | 0 |

Read paragraph 9 again.

19. How does paragraph 9 link to paragraph 7?

_____

_____

| 2 | 1 | 0 |

20. (*a*) **In your own words,** explain how the narrator lost his mother.

_____

| 2 | ■ | 0 |

(*b*) **In your own words,** explain how Hassan lost his mother.

_____

| 2 | ■ | 0 |

21. **In your own words,** what would most Afghans think about what Hassan's mother did?

_____

_____

| 2 | ■ | 0 |

Think about the passage as a whole.

22. This extract comes from the opening of the novel *The Kite Runner* which tells the story of how the narrator betrays Hassan and loses his friendship. In your opinion, is this an effective opening? Answer fully, quoting from the passage to support your answer.

_____

_____

| 2 | 1 | 0 |

English   Standard Grade: Credit

Practice Papers
For SQA Exams

Credit Level
Exam F
Reading

Answer all of the questions.

Read the following passage and then answer the questions. Remember to use your own words as much as possible.

The Hungry Ghosts

In Anne Berry's novel The Hungry Ghosts, *Alice Safford is an English girl living in Hong Kong with her family. Lin Shui, a Chinese girl who was murdered twenty-five years previously, is now a ghost who decides to 'possess' Alice. Lin Shui is the narrator of this section of the novel.*

1   I watch many children come and go before Alice arrives. I observe them through the grid of an air-vent set high into the wall of the morgue. Their heads are dull and ordinary and I know they cannot sustain me. True, I am curious. But when Alice comes I am spellbound. She appears one afternoon when all the other children have gone, and lies back on a patch of scrubby grass. She is a slip of a thing, pale as a creaming wave, her long hair always moving, her eyes moons of contemplation. It does not seem to worry her that the building above her is growing silent, that soon she will be alone. For a bit she stares up at the sky, follows the occasional fleecy cloud. Then she rolls over and sits up.

2   Suddenly she notices the yawning mouth of the morgue for the door is partly ajar. I cannot tell how long her eyes are trained on it, but the shadows are lengthening when at last she climbs to her feet. She walks straight to the entrance and shoulders open the rusty-hinged door. It shudders and grumbles and sticks a bit before swinging back. Alice slips through under the nebulous mantle. She takes a few steps, and then waits for her eyes to adjust to the gloom. She inhales a long, slow breath of stale, dead air. She fixes stains on the floor with her perceptive eyes. She lets her fingers linger on walls where the paint is flaking, where the bricks are impregnated with the transience of life. As she listens to echoes of the past, I slide into her and instantly feel my strength returning. I become the scum in her blood. I garland myself with ropes of silver-stranded veins. And in the resonance of each heartbeat I know her every thought, her every memory, her every experience, her every twist and turn of emotion, often before she does, as if they are my own.

3   When at last she leaves I go with her. We dawdle along Bowen Road. We wait for the Peak Tram, the funicular green cab with a cream roof to come and haul us up The Peak. We leave the terminus and stroll up a long road, past a shop called the Dairy Farm, then along a path to Alice's home. All this is new to me. The people hurrying by, their clothes, their colour too, for up here most of them are white-skinned, the cars and buses and lorries, the houses and the flats. Hers is a top-floor flat as large as a palace. Surely, I think, several families live here. But I am wrong. There is only one. The flat is filled with beautiful things too, the kind that an emperor might own. Carvings and paintings, jade and ivory, snuff bottles and fans, books and carpets, and shelves crowded with fine porcelain. But there is no emperor, just Alice's family, the Saffords, and some servants to care for them, Ah Dang and Ah Lee. When I was alive there was only my father to care for me. And even then, as far back as I can recall, it had really been my job to look after him. Like me, Alice has a father, Ralph, but unlike me she has a mother too, Myrtle. And Alice has a younger brother, Harry and a small dog she calls Bear. Alice has two sisters as well, who are being educated in England. It seems strange to me that, with so many people about, Alice should be lonely. But she is. I feel it. Still, it is lucky, because it means that she will probably welcome my company.

4   The flat on The Peak is emptier than I thought it would be, reminding me sometimes of the morgue. Alice's father is rarely at home, working constantly. Alice's mother, though sometimes in the same room, feels far away. I am envious of Alice having not one but two sisters. But I find even this, when they return home for the holidays, is not as I imagined it. Late one night we chance upon Jillian in the kitchen. She is surrounded by tins and packets and jars. She is stuffing food into her mouth, slices of bread slathered in chocolate spread and jam and peanut butter, cramming in biscuits and cakes and crisps and chocolate. In between mouthfuls she is gulping juice and milk, and brightly coloured drinks that bubble and fizz, as if infused with life force. I amuse myself by causing one of the tube lights in the kitchen to flash for a time. Jillian barely glances up. Instead, as it flickers, Alice's oldest sister looks as if she is jerking about like a gluttonous puppet, her blonde hair flying. Alice is po-faced but I think it is very funny.

5   All the while, fearless nocturnal cockroaches scuttle about. Emerging from the drains they feast on smears and crumbs. Most are on the floor, though a few, braver than the rest, scrabble around on the work surfaces. Their antennae swivel. They are well fed these cockroaches, the size of Hong-Kong dollars. Their beetle-brown bodies gleam in the glow cast by the fluorescent tubes. Fine hairs sprout from their busy, spindly legs. The wings of one that is trying to clamber up the slippery sides of a glass whirr madly. It lumbers into the air and flies about, rebounding off cupboard doors and tiled surfaces, before landing to gobble afresh on a fast-melting square of chocolate. They look as shiny as vinyl. Alice flinches. Jillian pauses in her gorging, just long enough to bring a clenched fist down on it. We hear the 'squish' as its mushy body is crushed. Jillian glances cursorily at the base of her fist. She wipes off the stuff that looks like yellow pus on a kitchen towel, and starts guzzling again.

morgue: a building in which dead bodies are kept
nebulous: hazy, cloudy, indistinct
mantle: door frame
transience: temporary nature
The Peak: the highest mountain in Hong Kong

Read paragraph 1 again.

		Marks	

1. Where and when does Lin Shui first see Alice?

   _____

   _____   2 | 1 | 0

2. Is Lin Shui interested in the children she sees before Alice arrives? Quote to support your answer.

   _____

   _____   2 | 1 | 0

3. Explain **in your own words** why Lin Shui might be 'spellbound' by Alice. Give **two** different reasons.

   (i) _____

   (ii) _____   2 | 1 | 0

4. Comment fully on the effectiveness of the image 'pale as a creaming wave'.

   _____

   _____   2 | 1 | 0

Read paragraph 2 again.

5. Comment on the author's word choice in the phrase 'the yawning mouth of the morgue'.

   _____

   _____   2 | 1 | 0

6. Write down **two** pieces of evidence from paragraph 2 which show that the door to the morgue was difficult to open.

   (i) _____

   (ii) _____   2 | 1 | 0

	Marks	

7. What mood or atmosphere does the writer create when describing the inside of the morgue? Give evidence from the passage to support your answer.

_____

_____

2 1 0

8. Comment fully on the effectiveness of the writer's word choice in the sentence 'I become the scum in her blood.'

_____

_____

2 1 0

9. Comment on the effectiveness of the writer's word choice in 'And in the resonance of each heartbeat I know her every thought, her every memory, her every experience, her every twist and turn of emotion, often before she does, as if they are my own.'

_____

_____

2 1 0

Read paragraph 3 again.

10. Write down **three** pieces of evidence from the beginning of paragraph 3 which show that the journey to Alice's home takes some time.

(i) _____

(ii) _____

(iii) _____

2 1 0

11. 'All this is new to me.' In your opinion, why might everything be 'new' to Lin Shui?

_____

_____

2 ■ 0

12. How are Lin Shui's parents and Alice's parents different?

_____

_____

2 1 0

Marks

13. **In your own words,** explain how Lin Shui feels about Alice being lonely. Quote from the passage to support your answer.

_____

_____

2 | 1 | 0

Read paragraph 4 again.

14. Why does Alice's flat remind Lin Shui of the morgue?

_____

_____

2 | 1 | 0

15. What is the function of the sentence 'But I find even this, when they return home for the holidays, is not as I imagined it.'?

_____

_____

2 | ■ | 0

16. How effective is the description of the way Jillian is eating in the sentence 'She is stuffing food into her mouth, slices of bread slathered in chocolate spread and jam and peanut butter, cramming in biscuits and cakes and crisps and chocolate.'?

_____

_____

2 | 1 | 0

17. How does Lin Shui react to the sight of Jillian's eating and drinking and why? Quote from the passage to support your answer.

_____

_____

2 | 1 | 0

18. Comment on the effectiveness of the simile 'like a gluttonous puppet'.

_____

_____

2 | 1 | 0

19. How does Alice react while she is watching Jillian's eating and drinking? Quote from the passage to support your answer.

_____

_____

2 1 0

Read paragraph 5 again.

20. (a) Identify and explain **one** technique used by the author to describe the cockroaches' behaviour.

_____

_____

2 1 0

(b) Identify and explain **one** technique used by the author to describe the cockroaches' appearance.

_____

_____

2 1 0

21. How does Jillian feel about killing the cockroach? Quote from the passage to support your answer.

_____

_____

2 1 0

Now think about the passage as a whole

22. Give **two** reasons why you think Alice might welcome being taken over by Lin Shui.

(i) _____

(ii) _____

2 1 0

23. Elsewhere in the novel, other characters become narrators, for example, Alice's mother, Alice and other ghosts. In your opinion, why has the author chosen to use Lin Shui as the narrator in this section?

_____

_____

2 ■ 0

24. Keeping secrets is an important theme in the novel. What evidence is there in this passage that secrets may become an important theme?

_____

_____

2 ■ 0

English   Standard Grade: Foundation, General and Credit

Practice Papers
For SQA Exams

Foundation, General and Credit Level
Writing

Read these instructions first.

1. Use the photographs and words to help you think about what to write. Look at it all and consider carefully all possibilities.

2. There are 21 questions to choose from.

3. Decide which **one** you will answer.
   Then write the number in the margin of your answer.

4. Think carefully abut the wording of your chosen answer.
   Make a **plan** before you start writing.
   Re-read your answer before you finish.
   Mark any changes **neatly**.

Scotland's leading educational publishers

PRACTICE WRITING PAPER

FIRST   Look at the photograph below. It shows a busy tourist resort.

NEXT   Think about being on holiday.

1.   Write about a memorable holiday. Remember to include your thoughts and feelings as well as describing your holiday experiences.

2.   Write a short story about someone on the holiday of a lifetime. You should develop setting, character and plot.

3.   Write a letter of complaint to a travel company about poor holiday accommodation.

4.   Write in any way you like about the picture.

FIRST   Look at the photograph below. It shows a school pupil in uniform.

NEXT   Think about school.

5. Are your schooldays the 'happiest days of your life'? Write about your experience of school. Remember to include your thoughts and feelings.

6. Write a short story using the following title: 'The School Bully'. You should develop setting, character and plot.

7. Many pupils in Scotland have to wear school uniform to school. Give your views.

8. 'Too Cool for School'. Write in any way you like using this title.

FIRST   Look at the photograph below. It shows children searching through rubbish for food or items they can sell.

NEXT   Think about the developing world.

9. Write a short story using the following opening:

    '*The children slipped as they climbed to the top, shouting to the little ones to hurry up and clawing at the stinking rubbish …*'

10. Write about how you make a contribution to helping others in this country or in the developing world.

11. Write an article for your school newspaper or magazine about any aspect of the environment, for example, global warming or pollution.

12. Write in any way you like about the picture.

FIRST   Look at the photograph below. It shows a family enjoying a birthday party in a restaurant.

NEXT   Think about celebrations.

13. Describe a memorable family occasion. Remember to include your thoughts and feelings.

14. Write a short story about uninvited guests at a party. You should develop setting, character and plot.

15. The Scottish Government has banned smoking in public places such as restaurants. Give your views.

The following questions do not have any photographs.

16. Watching too much television is bad for you. Give your views.

17. 'We All Make Mistakes.' Write in any way you like about this title.

18. Bill Shankly, a famous football club manager, once said 'Some people think football is a matter of life and death. I assure you it's much more serious than that.' Write in any way you like about football or any other sport.

19. Describe the scene brought to mind by one of the following:

    'I look at the night
    and make nothing of it –
    those black pages
    with no print.'

    OR

    'So many summers and I have lived them too.'

20. Write a short story in which the main character makes a mistake. You should develop setting and character as well as plot.

21. 'As a teenager I was so insecure. I was convinced I had absolutely no talent at all.' (Johnny Depp)

    Write about an experience you have had where you overcame your insecurity or demonstrated a talent.

1.   'Disengaged' suggests that they do not like school/are badly behaved/find school boring/are not interested in learning/are not motivated (2).

EXPLANATION

This question refers to the first sentence of the article. You are being asked in this question to explain the word 'disengaged' in your own words. Look at the answer for different ways of explaining this word.

Did you know the meaning of 'disengaged'? If not, you could guess the meaning from the rest of the sentence because you are told that 'disengaged' pupils say teachers are so boring, they send them to sleep!

GENERAL ADVICE

Questions will usually follow the order of the passage. So, the first questions will usually ask you about the first few sentences of the passage. Then the questions will work through the passage chronologically (in order).

Examiners write questions in this way to make things easier for you – so you will not have to jump around the passage to find the answers you are looking for! Usually, the examiner will help you to locate the answer by telling you where to look, for example, 'Read paragraph 1 again.'

2.   'Drop off' is an informal/colloquial/slang phrase (1).
AND
It has been used as this is a newspaper article/so that the article will appeal to young people/to create a conversational tone/to create humour (1).

EXPLANATION

Did you know that 'drop off' is informal? A more formal phrase might be 'fall asleep'. Informal language is used in some newspaper articles so that the tone is more 'chatty' or personal or conversational.

Here you gain one mark for identifying the informal tone and one mark for clearly explaining why it has been used.

GENERAL ADVICE

At General level, you will be expected to recognise formal and informal words and phrases. A good way to do this is to read newspaper articles just like this one. Quality newspapers such as the *Scotsman* or the *Glasgow Herald* normally use formal language. So, if you spot an informal or slang word in this type of newspaper article, it is likely that the writer has chosen it for a reason or to create a particular effect. Look at the suggested answer for some of the reasons writers use informal language.

Informal language can include:

- slang words/phrases
- words/phrases in dialect
- abbreviations
- ungrammatical structure or punctuation

3.   How to 'avoid distractions' (1).
AND
How to 'wind down' (1).

EXPLANATION

You know you are looking for two reasons as there are two marks available and you are asked for two pieces of evidence. If you only write one correct reason, you will only gain one mark.

'Write down evidence from the passage' usually means you should quote. Remember to use quotation marks to show these are words from the passage and not your own words.

The answer comes after the phrase 'to provide lessons for secondary pupils on how to'. Use a highlighter to highlight key words and phrases. This can help you focus on exactly where the answer is in the passage.

GENERAL ADVICE

Understanding questions ask you about ideas or information in the passage. This is one of the main types of question – there will always be a number of understanding questions. These questions are checking whether you have understood the ideas in the passage – what it is all about.

To answer understanding questions, first work out what the question is asking. Then find the answer in the passage. These questions usually ask you to answer in your own words, but not always, so be sure to check.

4.   The council is concerned because the problem is getting worse/there are more and more pupils with this problem (1).
AND
The pupils cannot achieve in school/do well in school/are not calm or ready to learn (1).

EXPLANATION

There are two main ideas in the sentence beginning 'The council is concerned …' The first idea is that the problem is increasing so you gain one mark for writing that the problem is getting worse or that more pupils seem to have this problem than previously. The second mark is for explaining the phrase 'to be able to learn, relax and be happy' in your own words.

As with question 3, some pupils find it helpful to underline or highlight key words in the questions to help them focus on what is being looked for. In this question, the key phrase is 'The council is concerned …' So you know that you are looking for reasons for this – the reasons are given in the phrases and sentences directly after this phrase. You could highlight this phrase or the ideas that come after it.

5.   Paragraph 2 word: 'unique' (1).
Paragraph 3 phrase: 'new pilot scheme' (1).

EXPLANATION

Always look at the words or phrases before a word as well as those which come after it to help you work out the meaning. Here the word 'unique' comes directly before 'project'. In paragraph 3, the word 'scheme' is used and the adjectives 'new' and 'pilot' come directly before it. So you could make a guess, even if you did not know these words. Unique means only or special and pilot means trial or experimental.

GENERAL ADVICE

What should you do if you don't know the meaning of a word? Here is the best way to work it out.

Context means the surrounding words and phrases. You should look at the context of the word because it may contain words or phrases which have a similar meaning or which can help you work out the meaning of the word or phrase. Remember that the context refers to all the words and phrases just before and just after the word or phrase in question.

6.   The words between the dashes add extra information to the sentence (2).
OR
The actual/specific names of the schools are given between the dashes (2).

EXPLANATION

Dashes are usually used for the same reason as brackets – to show that further information has been added to what has already been written. Here, the phrase 'four schools' is used just before the first dash and the information after the first dash adds detail by giving the names of the schools.

GENERAL ADVICE

You can learn how to answer punctuation questions quite easily by knowing about the uses of various punctuation marks – here are some examples.

- comma – to separate items in a list
- semi-colon – to separate items/phrases within a sentence
- colon or dash – to introduce an explanation or example
- two dashes – to separate a phrase which usually contains additional information
- brackets – to separate a phrase which usually contains additional information

7. Grade B teenagers get more sleep/11 minutes' more sleep than students who achieve Grade C (1).
OR
Grade B teenagers get less sleep/15 minutes' less sleep than students who achieve Grade A.
AND
Grade C teenagers get much less sleep than students who achieve Grade A (1).
OR
Grade C teenagers get less sleep than students who achieve Grade B (1).
OR
Grade C teenagers get the least sleep (1).

EXPLANATION

The phrase to look at closely is '. . . A grade teenagers had on average 15 minutes' more sleep every night than those students mainly achieving Bs, who in turn averaged 11 minutes' more than those at level C.' Did you work out that those who get most sleep have the highest academic achievement?

As always, highlighting key words and phrases may help. You could highlight the numbers given or the comparison phrases such as 'more than'.

GENERAL ADVICE

Like questions 1 and 3, this is an understanding question. Always read the question carefully, then read the relevant section of the passage carefully. Use the marks given to help you work out how much to write. Here you are given an idea about how much to write as one answer is done for you. Did this help you with writing the other two answers?

8. (*a*) 'Macho' suggests that getting very little sleep is something to be proud of/to boast about/is something manly/masculine/virile/tough (2).

(*b*) 'Virtue' suggests that getting very little sleep is a good thing/is positive/is admirable/is to be encouraged (2).

EXPLANATION

Did you know the meanings of 'macho' and 'virtue'? A 'virtue' is a positive characteristic or behaviour such as honesty or kindness. 'Macho' means 'very masculine'. You will gain two marks for giving the correct meaning of 'macho' and two marks for giving the correct meaning of 'virtue'.

GENERAL ADVICE

Another reason to read quality newspapers as often as you can when preparing for Standard Grade English is to learn new words. (Keep a dictionary beside you and look them up!) Learning new words will help you in Close Reading – sometimes it is very difficult to guess the meaning of a word. If you already knew the meaning of 'macho' and 'virtue', you are well on the way to four marks!

9. (i) 'emotional wellbeing' (or so that people feel well spiritually/mentally/emotionally) (1).
(ii) 'physical wellbeing' (or so that people feel well physically/feel healthy) (1).
(iii) 'memories are processed' (or 'brain can store the learning' or so that people can memorise/remember what they have learned) (1).

EXPLANATION

You are asked here for three reasons but there are only two marks available. It works like this:

three correct reasons = 2 marks
two correct reasons = 1 mark
one correct reason = 0 marks

Did you notice that you are not asked to write in your own words? So that means you can quote directly from the passage or use your own words. Look at the suggested answer for ways to explain these phrases in your own words.

10. She uses a rhetorical question to make the reader think about what she has said/to emphasise the importance of getting enough sleep (2).

EXPLANATION

Jane Ansell asks a rhetorical question – that is, a question which does not require an answer. By asking a question, a writer or speaker encourages the reader or listener to think about what their answer would be. It is as if Jane Ansell is speaking directly to you, the reader, and asking you a question. So this encourages you to think about your answer! You will gain two marks for correctly explaining why it has been used.

---

11. 'Sleep is when the brain rewires and consolidates the memory.'(2)

EXPLANATION

Highlighting will help you with this answer, especially as you are looking at two different paragraphs. Look for the word 'memory' in what Jane Ansell says. She repeats the idea that learning is processed and stored during sleep.

---

12. Sleeping can be taught in manageable chunks/one thing at a time/slowly/stage by stage (1) and by praising children/encouraging children/not scolding children (1).

EXPLANATION

You are being asked to explain the sentence '. . . sleeping can be taught, if it is broken down into achievable steps and is positively enforced . . .' You gain one mark for explaining 'broken down/achievable steps' and one mark for explaining 'positively enforced'.

---

13. In paragraph 10 we are told that Professor Munn 'believes' (1) that poor sleep patterns contribute to poor behaviour which shows that she agrees with this (1).
    OR
    We are told in paragraph 10 that Professor Munn 'supports' (1) the teaching of good sleep behaviour which shows that she approves of it/agrees with it (1).
    OR
    In paragraph 11, Professor Munn says 'It is very plausible that sleep deprivation and poor diet can contribute ...' (1) which shows that she believes/thinks this is likely (1).

EXPLANATION

A speaker's attitude or stance is clear through the words and ideas he/she chooses. Here you gain one mark for quoting a word or phrase Professor Munn uses and one mark for explaining how this shows her attitude.

There are three words to choose from here: 'believes', 'supports' or 'plausible'. Did you spot all three?

---

14. Her research shows that lack of sleep means many/a large number/lots of pupils (1) are unpleasant to each other/fight/argue/attack/abuse others (1).

EXPLANATION

This is another understanding question which asks you to explain '. . . quite a high percentage of pupil-to-pupil relationships, all over the school and in the classroom, have a degree of verbal and physical aggression' in your own words.

Use the highlighting technique to find and highlight two points about the research in paragraph 11. You know there are two marks available so you can work out that there is one mark for each correct point.

---

15. The sentence is a linking sentence (1).

AND

It refers back to information in previous paragraphs about how lack of sleep affects behaviour and memory/the paragraphs following describe the 'other impacts' of lack of sleep (1).

EXPLANATION

'What is the function of this sentence?' means 'What does this sentence **do**?'

In this case, the sentence is a linking sentence. It **refers back** to the previous paragraphs and **introduces** a new idea. Did you notice how many marks are available here? For full marks, you have to identify that this is a linking sentence. Then you should explain that this sentence refers back or that it introduces a new idea – the other impacts that lack of sleep can have – which the writer then goes on to explore.

GENERAL ADVICE

You may be asked at General level to explain the function of a word, phrase or sentence. For example, you could be asked about the function of a sentence at the beginning or at the end of a paragraph (sometimes called a topic sentence) or the function of a single word.

The function of a word or phrase can be to

- summarise
- explain
- show a result
- show a contrast
- give an example
- link with what has gone before or what comes after

There is sometimes a key word or phrase which 'signals' the function to you. However, there is sometimes no 'signal' word or phrase to help you work out the function – you have to work this out from the words of the sentence itself.

Look at the linking words and phrases below – can you work out their functions?

- in short
- furthermore
- the former ... the latter ...
- besides
- since
- as a result
- nonetheless
- unlike
- however

---

16. Lack of sleep means children are more likely to be/have more chance of being depressed/miserable/down/bad tempered (1).

AND

Lack of sleep means that doctors or teachers or psychologists may incorrectly think that a child has Attention Deficit Hyperactivity Disorder (ADHD)/autism/medical/behaviour problems (1).

EXPLANATION

From paragraph 13, you gain one mark for identifying that those who get less sleep are at 'higher risk of depression'. So you could write that children are more likely to be miserable.

In paragraph 14, there is a lot of information about misdiagnosis of ADHD and autism; in other words, professionals sometimes think children who do not get enough sleep may have medical or psychological issues. Did you know that 'misdiagnosis' means a wrong diagnosis?

---

17. Any two from:

Spend time with the family earlier in the evening (1).

AND/OR

Remove technology and gadgets from children's bedrooms (1).

AND/OR

Make sure children go to bed early (1).

EXPLANATION

In paragraph 15, we are told that children may go to bed late because parents coming home from work want to spend time with their families. Spending time with children at other times or coming home earlier might have an effect.

In paragraph 16, clearing bedrooms of gadgets is mentioned – so removing technology might have an effect.

Take care to use your own words. Always check that you have not copied any words from the passage.

---

18. She dislikes technology in teenagers' bedrooms (1) as she uses the word 'invaded' which means 'attacked' or 'took over' (1).

OR

She dislikes technology in teenagers' bedrooms (1) as we are told she wants bedrooms 'cleared' of technology (1).

OR

She dislikes technology in teenagers' bedrooms (1) as she thinks allowing technology makes it 'more difficult' for parents (1).

EXPLANATION

An attitude or stance is shown by the words and ideas the writer or speaker uses. Take care with this question – you are asked about Jane Ansell's attitude. Technology is described as a 'bugbear' – that is, something that is annoying. These are the journalist's words and not a quote from Jane Ansell. Look at the sentence starting 'When Ansell is working with families' and at what she is quoted as saying to work out how she feels about technology. There are three different words or phrases to choose from.

Quote for one mark and explain for one mark.

19. The phrase/image/metaphor 'fed, watered and rested' usually refers to pets/animals (1) which have to be cared for in the same way as parents care for children/which need the same care as children/so he is comparing animals to children as they both need care (1).

EXPLANATION

Did you spot that this is a metaphor? The phrase 'fed and watered' is usually used about horses or cattle so Ronnie Smith is comparing children to animals. You will gain one mark for explaining that this phrase is usually used to refer to animals and not children. You do not need to use the word 'metaphor' but you must recognise that this is an image or a comparison to gain two full marks.

GENERAL ADVICE

You will always be asked about the writer's word choice, language and structure.

When you are asked about word choice, you should analyse the language the writer uses – why he/she has chosen particular words/phrases/images.

When answering, many pupils explain only what a word, phrase or sentence **means**. You should explain what it means **and** why it has been used/is effective to gain full marks.

20. Make the most of their time at school/learn as much as they can/achieve the marks they deserve/ stretch themselves academically (2).

EXPLANATION

To gain two marks, you should explain the word 'maximising' which means getting the most out of something and 'learning potential' which means what it is possible to learn or what someone is capable of learning. Did you notice that there are only two marks or no marks available? This is because the answer only has 1 part – giving the meaning of the phrase.

GENERAL ADVICE

This phrase is an example of jargon. Jargon is language used by a specific group or profession which others may not understand. For example, teachers may talk about you 'achieving your learning potential' – what they really mean is you being the very best you can be!

21. This is an effective title (1) because it is a pun/play on words about the difficulty of getting to sleep (1).

OR

This is an effective title (1) as it summarises what the passage is about which is the difficulty of getting teenagers to sleep more (1).

OR

This is not an effective title (1) as it is imaginative but the article is very factual/informative (1).

EXPLANATION

This is an evaluation question because it asks for your opinion – the key phrase in the question is 'Do you think ...?' Of course, your answer must be based on your understanding of the title and the passage. Did you know that describing something as 'a dream' means it may never happen?

You can suggest that the title is not effective if this is your opinion. You will gain one mark for explaining whether it is or is not effective and one mark for a valid reason.

GENERAL ADVICE

Questions which ask for your opinion can be called 'evaluation' questions. In other words, you are being asked to make a judgement. Don't forget, though, that you have to back up your opinion with reasons. In your answer, you could use phrases such as:

- in my opinion . . .
- I feel . . .
- I think . . .
- my view is . . .
- I agree/disagree that . . .

---

22. Parents are most likely to read the article (1) as they may have problems with their children sleeping and the passage includes advice for them (1).

OR

Pupils are most likely to read this article (1) as they may have difficulty sleeping and want more information about this (1).

OR

Teachers are most likely to read this article (1) as they may want to know more about how to help pupils with sleeping problems (1).

EXPLANATION

This is another evaluation question asking for your opinion. You can see from the suggested answers that you can choose any reader as long as you explain your reasons clearly. Which reader did you choose? You gain one mark for identifying who is most likely to read the article and one mark for a valid explanation.

GENERAL ADVICE

The potential readers of a text can be described in different ways – look at the examples below. If any of these phrases are used in a question, you know that you are being asked about who might read the passage.

'Intended readership' or 'readership' or 'readers' or 'potential readers'.

'Target audience' or 'audience' or 'intended audience' or 'potential audience'.

All texts have an intended audience and purpose (question 23 gives you more information about purpose). Experienced writers decide on their audience and purpose before they start writing. Then when they write, they make choices about ideas, language and structure based on who they are writing for and why they are writing.

23. The purpose is to argue for giving school pupils sleeping lessons (1) because the writer includes many reasons why sleep is important (1).

EXPLANATION

Writers always have a purpose in writing. Think about why the writer has written about the sleeping lessons project. The passage informs us about the importance of sleep but does more than that. It also contains many ideas in support of sleeping lessons; for example, information from several experts.

GENERAL ADVICE

Often, a writer has more than one purpose. Look at the list below – can you work out if the writer of this passage has more than one of these purposes?

- to entertain
- to persuade
- to express feelings
- to inform
- to describe
- to reflect
- to argue
- to explain
- to report

24. The writer uses examples of research/statistics (1) which support the need for teenagers to get plenty of sleep/which show that getting more sleep means higher grades/which show that lack of sleep is sometimes misdiagnosed (1).
OR
The writer interviews several experts/uses their words/quotes what they say (1) to support the argument for the importance of sleep for teenagers (1).

EXPLANATION

You are being asked in this question about one of the writer's techniques – this means something the writer does. Did you realise that the writer had added quotes and statistics to 'add weight' which means to back up or justify or give evidence for what he is writing? You gain one mark for correctly identifying a technique and one mark for a valid reason why the writer has used this technique.

GENERAL ADVICE

Journalists use techniques such as interviews and statistics to try to persuade you about a topic. Other ways of persuading a reader include:

- using emotive/strong language, for example, exaggeration, repetition, rhetorical questions
- using examples or anecdotes
- using structure to organise ideas for and against

PRACTICE EXAM D   CREDIT LEVEL WORKED ANSWERS

1. His impression is that the school is noisy/busy/crowded (1) **or** he feels alone/lonely (1).
   '. . . charging around shouting'/'amid the din'/'brief hug'/'then they're gone' (1).

EXPLANATION

This is an 'understanding' question. This means it asks you to explain ideas or information from the passage. The first question is usually not too difficult!

You are also asked to quote from the paragraph. Understanding questions often ask you to quote to show where you have found the answer.

GENERAL ADVICE

Questions will usually follow the order of the passage. So, the first questions will usually ask you about the first few sentences or paragraphs of the passage. Then the questions will work through the passage chronologically (in the order that the events happened).

Examiners write questions in this way to make things easier for you – so you will not have to jump around the passage to find the answers you are looking for! Sometimes, the examiner will help you to locate the answer by telling you where to look, for example, 'Read paragraph 1 again.'

2. The reader feels as though the action is happening now/makes the events seem faster/quicker/more direct/keeps the reader more interested (2).

EXPLANATION

This is an analysis question which means it asks you about the language the writer has chosen. You are being asked why the writer has used present tense. Remember that tense refers to the use of verbs. Writers usually use present tense to make it seem to the reader as if the action is happening now. You will gain two full marks for a correct answer!

GENERAL ADVICE

You will always be asked about the writer's word choice, language and structure.

When you are asked about word choice, you should analyse the language the writer uses – why he/she has chosen particular words/phrases/images.

When answering, many pupils explain only what a word, phrase or sentence **means**. You should explain what it means **and** why it has been used/is effective to gain full marks.

3. The writer feels anonymous/not special/not an individual/that his name is not important (2).

EXPLANATION

This is another understanding question – most candidates find these the easiest to answer as you are simply being asked to understand and explain ideas in the passage.

Remember that highlighting or underlining key words or phrases in the question can help. The phrase 'in your own words' is used here, so you cannot quote from the passage and must answer in your own words.

You will gain two full marks for a correct answer!

4. He has left behind his family/pets/belongings (1) and the ability to do what he likes/the right to do what he wanted (1).

EXPLANATION

Some pupils find it helpful to highlight words or phrases in the passage – either as they read through the passage for the first time or as they work through the questions. It's up to you. Highlighting can help you to find a word or phrase or idea. Here you could highlight the phrase 'I've left behind . . .'

Some pupils also find it useful to highlight words or phrases in the question. Here you could highlight 'left behind'. This can help you to focus on exactly what the question is asking you.

The highlighting technique can be very useful. Try it for yourself and see if it works for you.

5. They are in different dormitories/parts of the school (1): 'in other boarding houses' (1).
    OR
    '. . . our paths won't cross often' (1) tells me that they will not meet often (1).

EXPLANATION

You are being asked here to answer and quote from the passage. Look at the two suggested answers again – the first answer explains, then quotes. The second answer quotes first, then explains. Try answering in both ways and find out which order you prefer.

GENERAL ADVICE

There are different ways to ask you to quote from the passage. The word 'evidence' is often used. This is just another way of asking you to quote. Look at the phrases below and get to know them – they are all asking you to quote!

- Support your answer with evidence
- Quote from the passage
- Which word/phrase . . .?
- Using evidence
- Give an example
- Illustrate your answer (this does not mean draw a picture!)
- Refer closely to the passage
- Identify the word(s)
- Write down the word(s)
- What expression . . .?

6. His golf bag (with golf clubs and balls) (1). He feels it belongs to him/it is personal to him/it connects him to golf which he loves (1).

EXPLANATION

This understanding question asks you about the writer's golf bag. For full marks, you must explain the phrase 'This golf bag has no name tag on it, but at least it is mine' in your own words. It is important that you explain the idea that the bag belongs to him – earlier in the paragraph we are told that he has left many things behind and that he feels alone.

GENERAL ADVICE

Always look at the marks available to help you work out how many points to make/how much to write. Two marks usually means you should make two points. The words in the question will also help you so read carefully. Highlighting the key words or phrases in the question may help too.

7. (a) His two years at boarding school (2).

   (b) He is unsure/he guesses/assumes that everyone feels this way (1) – 'presumably' (1).

EXPLANATION

'[T]hose two years at boarding school' gives you the answer to question 7(a). To answer 7(b), you have to work out the meaning of 'presumably' and explain it. To presume means to guess. Did you know the meaning?

Look at question 8 below for help with how to work out the meaning of words you do not know.

8. 'Endured' means suffered or put up with something unpleasant or difficult (1).
   AND
   The phrase 'it was rotten' shows that he found school unpleasant /'I'd run away twice' shows that he disliked school (1).

EXPLANATION

The phrases 'it was rotten' and 'I'd run away twice' might help – did you notice that 'it was rotten' is in the sentence BEFORE the word and 'I'd run away twice' is in the sentence AFTER the word? Remember that the context refers to all the words and phrases just before and just after the word or phrase in question. You should always look before and after a word or phrase to try to work out its meaning.

9.   The writer uses a metaphor (1) to describe the memory which 'surfaces'. This is effective as his memories of school are hidden/he does not think about school often/he dismisses his memories (1).

EXPLANATION

This is an example of a question which asks you to analyse the writer's language. You are asked if you think the image is effective. You can say it is or is not effective as long as you give good clear reasons for your answer.

Did you notice there are two marks available here? You should identify the image for one mark, then explain why it is effective for the second mark.

Remember, whenever you are asked to explain an image you should:

- identify what two things/people are being compared
- state whether you think this is an effective comparison and why.

GENERAL ADVICE

You should expect a question about imagery, for example,

- a simile;
- a metaphor;
- personification.

You may be given the image or you may have to find it for yourself. You then have to comment on how effective it is. A technique some pupils find helpful is to list as many similarities as possible between the object/movement/action/feeling itself and the object/movement/action/feeling to which it is compared. The more similarities, the more effective the image!

10.   He feels they are telling the truth/talking honestly/not pretending or lying (1): 'in all sincerity' (1).

EXPLANATION

The writer's attitude or stance is clear through the words and ideas he chooses. Here the writer uses the phrase 'in all sincerity' which means that he thinks people are being honest when they are positive about boarding school. We already know the writer is not positive about boarding school. You will gain 1 mark for correctly identifying the writer's attitude and one mark for a valid quote.

GENERAL ADVICE

Remember that a writer always has an attitude to what he/she is writing whether the writing is fiction or non-fiction. It is sometimes easier to spot a writer's attitude in non-fiction because the writer can explain directly what he or she thinks or feels. In fiction, the writer's attitude is conveyed through the characters so it is sometimes more difficult to work out.

You can work out the writer's attitude by thinking carefully about the words he/she has chosen.

11.   This phrase introduces the specific incident in the games room (1) which the writer describes in detail in later paragraphs (1).

EXPLANATION

You may be asked about the function of a sentence, phrase, word or idea. Here you are asked about a phrase. The function of a phrase means what it is for – not what it means!

The key words here are 'I see the games room'. This phrase gives the first mention of the games room which the writer then describes in detail in the paragraphs following. So this is a linking phrase which introduces a new idea.

GENERAL ADVICE

A sentence may contain a word or phrase which refers back to a previous idea or forward to a new idea. This is what is called 'linking'.

Authors sometimes use 'linking words' which make this easier to spot! Look out for linking words and phrases such as:

- however
- although
- despite
- in addition
- furthermore.

12. They appeared/seemed to the writer to be strong/un-stoppable/invincible (1) but they were young/spotty/adolescent/skinny (1).

EXPLANATION

In understanding questions, it can be helpful to highlight key words and phrases. Here you could highlight on the question paper the words 'then' and 'now'. You could also highlight these words in the passage itself. Highlighting can help you to focus on where to look for an answer.

Read the question carefully – it tells you that the writer has different feelings then and now. You know you are looking for two points. Check the marks available – one mark for what he thought then and one mark for what he thinks now. Working through the question logically will help you!

13. The boys knew something was going to happen (1): 'The door was shut, the table tennis table moved aside.'/'We were commanded to line up against the far wall, facing out.' (1)
OR
The boys knew there might be violence (1): 'Some heavy leather footballs were brought out.' (1)

EXPLANATION

In paragraph 8 there are several reasons why the boys were silent. You are asked for your opinion which means there is no wrong answer as long as you can quote from the passage to back up what you have written.

GENERAL ADVICE

Questions which ask for your opinion can be called 'evaluation' questions. In other words, you are being asked to make a judgement. You can use your general knowledge to help you answer.

Don't forget, though, that you have to back up your opinion with reasons.

14. Technique: *word choice* (1). 'Red-faced'/'terrorizing'/'god-like' shows the writer feels the head of house is frightening (1).
OR
Technique: *rhetorical questions* (1). The list of questions shows that the writer is very interested to know/still wonders/wants the reader to think about what the head of house is like as an adult (1).

EXPLANATION

In word choice questions, you should comment on:

- the specific words the writer has used/the technique(s) used

and

- the effect of these words/techniques.

To gain full marks here, identify the technique in the first part of your answer. Then explain how the words show how the writer feels. For example, if someone is 'terrorising' then they are frightening you and if they are 'god-like' then they are very powerful.

Another technique used here is sentence structure. Did you know that a rhetorical question is a question that does not require an answer? The reader may think of his or her own answer though!

GENERAL ADVICE

You will always be asked to analyse the writer's craft at Credit level. In other words, you will be asked about decisions the writer has made about word choice, language and structure.

Word choice

When you are asked about word choice, you should analyse the language the writer uses – why he/she has chosen particular words/phrases/images.

When answering, many pupils explain only what a word, phrase or sentence **means**. You should explain what it means **and** why it has been used/is effective to gain full marks.

Structure

When you are asked about structure, you should analyse the structure of phrases, sentences, paragraphs, the whole passage – why he/she has used particular or unusual patterns, order, organisation, e.g.

how the writer has chosen to punctuate the sentence
or
how long or short the sentence is and why
or
the pattern of the sentence and why it has been written in this way.

When answering, many pupils explain only what a word, phrase or sentence **means**. You should explain what it means **and** why it has been used/is effective to gain full marks. You have to comment on the effect of the punctuation, length or pattern; in other words, what the structure does and not just what it looks like!

---

15. He may be unhappy in his marriage/he does not know his children/he is a drunk/he blames others (1).
AND
He may be good/caring/supportive/loved/happy in his relationships (1).

EXPLANATION

You are looking here for contrast – two different descriptions of the bully as an adult. The first suggestion the writer makes is that the bully is unhappy as an adult, that his wife is 'unfaithful', that his children are 'strangers', that he is a drunk.

The second suggestion the writer makes is that the bully becomes 'decent, useful . . . kind . . . loyal'; in other words, that he grows up differently.

GENERAL ADVICE

You are likely to be asked at General and Credit levels about contrasting ideas/information. Some words or phrases signal contrasting ideas, for example:

* however   • although   • but.

Sometimes there are no 'signal' words – it is the ideas themselves which are different.

---

16. Any one from:
One of the boys shouts 'Wait!' (1). This makes the reader realise something is about to happen/ it stops the action before it can move on/it makes the reader question why the writer must wait (1).
OR
The boy's actions are described – walked up, looked, carefully removed glasses, put them away (1). This builds up tension as this is a detailed, long description (1).
OR
By creating the idea of the writer's glasses being removed as they may be broken (1). This builds up tension as the reader knows a violent act is about to happen (1).
OR
The boy says 'You'll get these back later.' (1) This makes the reader question what is going to happen before the glasses are returned (1).

17. The older boys kicked footballs directly at the new boys (1).
     AND
     The new boys did not turn round or try to protect themselves (1).

18. The sentence is a list of verbs separated by commas (1). This is effective as it shows that the incident is chaotic/fast/the actions are happening all at the same time (1).

19. (a) He imagines the situation is not happening/he does not react/he tries to remove himself from the situation/he tries to hide from it until it stops (2).

     (b) 'I was still far away, lying by the river at the bottom of our garden.' (2)

20. They were slightly injured (1): 'a few bloody noses, bruises, shocks'/'no lasting physical damage' (1).

EXPLANATION

This is an understanding question. Did you find the answer in the sentences: 'Physical results; a few bloody noses, bruises, shocks and tears. No lasting physical damage of course but enough to break us in'? The key words in the question are 'physically injured' so you know you are looking for evidence of physical pain and not mental pain.

21. To make the new boys realise who was in control (2).

OR

To make the new boys realise that they could not question what happened to them at boarding school (2).

EXPLANATION

Look at the lines '. . . to break us in. To make it clear we no longer had any individual dignity, freedom, value. Here we would do what we were told because we were told, and take what was coming to us and not ask why.' You should put the idea of having no individual freedom into your own words for two marks. Think hard about how to use your own words so you do not copy any words from the passage.

22. One of the older boys/the head of house (1) who does not want any teachers to hear/does not want to hear the crying of the new boys/to increase his feeling of power (1).

OR

One of the new boys/the writer (1) who does not want any teachers to hear/is upset or annoyed by the sound of other boys crying (1).

OR

The writer (1) speaking to himself to stop the memories of such a painful experience (1).

EXPLANATION

You are not told who shouts this phrase. Think about who might have shouted it. Which people are present in the games room? We know there are no teachers or adults present. So the speaker must be one of the boys. Or it may be that these words are not shouted out loud; they may be words said in the writer's imagination.

GENERAL ADVICE

Questions which ask for your opinion can be called 'evaluation' questions. In other words, you are being asked to make a judgement.

Your opinion is never wrong – so it is OK to agree or disagree! Don't forget, though, that you have to back up your opinion with reasons – what teachers call 'evidence'. Remember that when you see the word 'evidence' in a Close Reading question, this means you have to quote or explain ideas from the passage. Only use evidence you have from other reading or knowledge or experience if you are specifically asked for this.

23. His purpose is to persuade the reader to agree that bullying is wrong (1): 'it is one of the many terrible things in our world that makes me angry' (1).

OR

His purpose is to persuade the reader to disagree with boarding schools (1): 'simply wretched' (1).

OR

His purpose is to describe his feelings and memories about a frightening bullying experience (1): 'it was rotten' (1).

EXPLANATION

Writers always have a purpose in writing. Think about why the writer has described the bullying incident; he describes it as a frightening experience and he explains how he feels bullying is wrong. So you can work out that he may be trying to persuade you that it is wrong. He also describes how he feels now about bullying so his purpose may be to 'make sense' of what happened to him as a child by describing and remembering it in detail. You will gain one mark for explaining his purpose and one mark for a quote which backs this up.

GENERAL ADVICE

Often, a writer has more than one purpose. Look at the list below – can you work out if the writer of this passage has more than one purpose?

- to entertain
- to inform
- to argue
- to explain
- to persuade
- to describe
- to express feelings
- to reflect
- to report

1. They were standing on stools and benches to reach the high windows (1) so they could watch the football match/see the playing field clearly (1).

EXPLANATION

Usually, the first question is not too difficult! Some pupils find it helpful to underline or highlight key words in the questions to help them to focus on what is being looked for. In this question, the key phrase is 'standing up on stools and benches'. So you know that you are looking for reasons for this – the reasons are given in the phrases and sentences directly after this: 'crowding around the high windows' and 'a clear view of the North Playing Field' and 'to play football'.

GENERAL ADVICE

Questions will usually follow the order of the passage. So, the first questions will usually ask you about the first few sentences or paragraphs of the passage. Then the questions will work through the passage chronologically (in the order that the events happened). Examiners write questions in this way to make things easier for you – so you will not have to jump around the passage to find the answers you are looking for!

2. Kathy reasons/thinks that it was raining earlier because the sun was sparkling/shining (1) on the wet grass/earth (1).

EXPLANATION

This is called an 'understanding' question – these ask you to explain ideas or information in the passage. Question 1 was also an 'understanding' question. Look after the phrase 'I can remember' to find 'how the sun was glinting on the muddy surface of the grass.' You have to use your own words so you cannot write 'glinting' or 'muddy' in your answer!

GENERAL ADVICE

You are asked to explain **in your own words** so you must not quote words directly from the passage. If the question doesn't specifically say whether to quote or use your own words, then do both!

3. So that the boys do not know/notice they are being watched (2).

EXPLANATION

In paragraph 2, did you spot the phrase 'Someone said we shouldn't be so obvious about watching'? The question asks you why someone suggests they should move away so you have to explain this phrase in your own words. Can you think of another way of saying this?

GENERAL ADVICE

Examiners ask you to quote in different ways. Look at the phrases below and get to know them – they are all asking you to quote!

- Quote from the passage
- Which word/phrase ...?
- Support your answer with evidence from the text
- Give an example
- Illustrate your answer (this does not mean draw a picture!)
- Write down evidence from the passage
- Refer closely to the passage
- Identify the word(s)
- Write down the word(s)
- What expression ...?

4. The writer uses repetition of 'doesn't suspect' (1) to emphasise that Tommy is completely
    unaware of what is about to happen (1).

EXPLANATION

To gain full marks, you have to identify what is unusual about the word choice – the writer repeats a phrase –
and comment on the **effect** of this repetition. The effect of a technique means what the technique **does**.

Here it **emphasises** Tommy's lack of awareness because the phrase 'he doesn't suspect a thing' is
repeated with the addition of 'really' which adds even more emphasis.

Remember that if you emphasise a word or phrase (for example, by repeating it), you make it stand out or
make it more important.

GENERAL ADVICE

Examiners often include questions on word choice. These are called 'analysis' questions –
questions which ask you to analyse the writer's craft. In other words, you will be asked about the
choices the writer has made regarding the language he or she uses.

When answering, many pupils fall into the trap of only explaining what the sentence **means**. You
should explain what it means **and** comment on the word choice **and** why it has been used/is
effective to gain full marks.

5. (i)   She does not show any 'signs of disapproval'.
    (ii) She 'gave a little laugh'.
    (iii) She calls Tommy an 'idiot'.

EXPLANATION

You are asked for evidence in this question. 'Write down evidence' from the passage usually means you
should quote. Remember to use quotation marks to show these are the words from the passage and not
your own words.

Work through the sentences and find ideas which show Ruth approves of what will happen. You can use
your general knowledge to help you answer this question as you know that people do not laugh or insult
others when they disapprove of something.

GENERAL ADVICE

Sometimes it is tricky to work out how marks are allocated! Here you are asked for three pieces of
evidence but there is a maximum of two marks. It works like this:

three pieces of evidence = 2 marks
two pieces of evidence = 1 mark
one piece of evidence = 0 marks

6. The girls knew that something had been planned (1).
    AND
    The girls were slightly interested in what was going to happen at the football match (1).

EXPLANATION

Look at the underlined phrases in the sentence '. . . *not because we relished the prospect of seeing Tommy get
humiliated* yet again, but just *because we'd heard about this latest plot* and were *vaguely curious to watch it unfold.'*

Can you match them with the sentences in the boxes? The only one which is false is 'the girls were looking
forward to seeing Tommy's embarrassment' because the writer tells us it was '<u>not</u> because we relished the
prospect . . .'

7. Detached (2)

EXPLANATION

Think about what 'remote' means – far away, distant, separate. 'Detached', which also means separate,
appears in the last sentence of the paragraph. Read right through the paragraph very carefully.

GENERAL ADVICE

Always have a go at a question. You may feel you have no idea what the answer is but if you write nothing, you will gain no marks! If you write an answer, you just might be correct so never leave an answer blank.

8. (i)   'rushing about that field' (1).

    (ii)   'undisguised delight' (1).

EXPLANATION

Did you remember that 'support your answer with evidence from the text' and 'write down evidence from the passage' both mean you should quote directly? The key word in the question is 'enjoying'. So you are looking for words or phrases which show Tommy's enjoyment.

You will gain one mark for each correct quote.

GENERAL ADVICE

Look back at question 3 for more advice on when you should quote.

9. He liked the shirt/it was bought recently (1). The shirt might be spoiled/get dirty/be torn/damaged (1).

EXPLANATION

The phrases 'the one he was so proud of' and 'his favourite polo shirt' and 'in the sales' tell you that Tommy liked his new shirt. The first part of the answer should explain this in the candidate's own words. Kathy's thoughts about Tommy being stupid and that the shirt would 'get ruined' give you the second part of the answer.

10. She was laughing at/making fun of him (1) by copying how Tommy was looking/what Tommy was doing (1).

EXPLANATION

We are told that Laura was 'the big clown' in the group so you can guess that she was laughing at or making fun of Tommy. The idea of laughing at him gains one mark. 'Mimicking' means 'copying' so the idea of copying gains one mark. Look at the answer to see the two parts.

11. The phrase is a list of verbs separated by commas (1). This shows how much Tommy was doing/that Tommy was very active/energetic in the game (1).

EXPLANATION

The writer uses a list of verbs to emphasise how involved Tommy was in the football game. He was running and waving and calling and tackling.

GENERAL ADVICE

When you are asked about structure, you should analyse the structure of phrases, sentences, paragraphs, the whole passage – why he/she has used particular or unusual patterns, order, organisation, e.g.

how the writer has chosen to punctuate the sentence
or
how long or short the sentence is and why
or
the pattern of the sentence and why it has been written in this way.

When answering, many pupils explain only what a word, phrase or sentence **means**. You should explain what it means **and** why it has been used/is effective to gain full marks. To gain full marks, you have to comment on the effect of the punctuation, length or pattern; in other words, what the structure does and not just what it looks like!

12. 'Quip' means a joke/funny remark (1). Kathy had said something which Ruth thought was a 'joke' and we are then told she 'made some quip of her own' so we know that she said something similar (1).

EXPLANATION

You gain one mark for giving the meaning of 'quip'. 'Some kind of joke' and 'laughed half-heartedly' both help you to work out that 'quip' means a joke or funny saying. Your explanation gives you the second part of the answer and the second mark.

GENERAL ADVICE

Context means the words and phrases round about the word or phrase itself. Look at the context of the word because this may contain words or phrases which have a similar meaning and they might help you work out the meaning of the word or phrase.

Remember that the context refers to all the words and phrases just before and just after. So 'joke' and 'laughed half-heartedly' might help – these come just before the phrase 'made some quip of her own'.

---

13. (a) <u>The other boys</u>
Any two from:
pretending they did not care/ignoring the process/doing other things/chatting/tying boots/ staring (1).

(b) <u>Tommy</u>
Any two from:
'Looking eagerly'/watching enthusiastically/waiting for his name to be called (1).

EXPLANATION

Did you notice that you are not asked to quote or use your own words in this question? So this time, you can choose which you prefer. Most candidates find it easier to quote. Which do you prefer?

There are two parts to the question. The first part asks you about the other boys and the second part asks you about Tommy. The first part comes from the sentence starting 'The other boys . . .' and the second part comes from the sentence starting 'But Tommy was . . .'

---

14. (i) enthusiastic, happy, keen, ready
(ii) worry, anxiety, uncertainty
(iii) offended, distressed, hysterical, frightened, terrified

---

EXPLANATION

There are two marks available for this question but you are asked for three different expressions.

three correct expressions = 2 marks

two correct expressions = 1 mark

one correct expressions = 0 marks

You should explain each of the expressions in your own words:

'bright eager'
'puzzled concern'
'hurt and panic'

Punctuation helps you here – did you notice each of the expressions is introduced by a colon or semi-colon?

---

15. 'Egging her on' means encouraging her (2).

EXPLANATION

This is another question which is asking you for the meaning of a word or phrase. It may be easier for you as you are given alternatives and you are asked to choose one of these. Read the phrase carefully in the passage to help you to work out what it might mean.

---

16. The last sentence is a list of numbers, counting down (1) which creates tension as the reader knows something is about to happen when number one is reached (1).

OR

The writer uses several very short sentences (1) which shows the speaker is excited/breathless/expectant (1).

OR

The writer refers to 'it' in the sentence 'It's coming' (1) which makes the reader question what 'it' is (1).

EXPLANATION

There are several possible answers here. You can answer on word choice or sentence structure so choose the one you are most comfortable with. You should identify the word choice or structure you are referring to for one mark – for example, very short sentences. Then you should explain how this creates tension for the second mark.

GENERAL ADVICE

Writers create tension in different ways:

- theme/content – a passage may be about an exciting/frightening/dangerous event
- word choice/imagery – writers use words to build up tension, for example, through description
- sentence structure/length/punctuation – writers use unusual structures, for example, one word sentences, exclamation marks

---

17. It is effective as the word 'thunderous' shows how loudly/forcefully/angrily Tommy shouted (2).

OR

It is effective as the word 'bellowing' compares the noise Tommy makes to that of a loud animal (2).

EXPLANATION

You can choose to answer on 'thunderous' or 'bellowing'. To gain two full marks, you should explain what the word tells you about the **way** in which Tommy shouted.

---

18. He stood 'glaring' (1) after the boys which means to stare very hard/intensely (1).

OR

His face was 'scarlet' (1) which means bright red (1).

OR

He began to 'scream and shout' (1) which shows how angry he was (1).

OR

His words were a 'nonsensical jumble' (1) which indicates he was very agitated/speaking very fast (1).

OR

He used 'swear words and insults' (1) which shows how angry he was (1).

EXPLANATION

Always read the question carefully – you are asked about Tommy's feelings **after** the boys run off. So the answer comes after the phrase 'started to run off'.

'By referring closely to the passage' means you should quote (look back at question 3 for more advice about when to quote). Look at the first parts of all the suggested answers to read all the quotes you could have used in your answer. Now look at the second parts of the answers – the second part explains how the word or phrase indicates Tommy's feelings are intense. In other words, that Tommy is very angry!

19. They had seen Tommy having tantrums before (1): 'seen plenty of Tommy's tantrums by then' (1).
OR
They wanted to change the subject (1): 'We tried to start up a conversation about something else' (1).

EXPLANATION

You are asked for your opinion in this question which means there is no wrong answer as long as you can quote from the passage to back up what you have written. As usual, quote for one mark and explain the quote for the second mark or vice versa.

GENERAL ADVICE

Remember that when you see the word 'evidence' in a Close Reading question, this means you have to quote from the passage.

20. They are used to separate the phrase 'probably a full ten minutes after we'd first moved away' which explains in more detail how much time had passed since the children had moved away from the window (2).

EXPLANATION

Dashes are used to separate a phrase which adds more detail, information or further explanation.

Did you notice the allocation of marks is the same as for question 15? You get two marks for giving the correct answer and no marks if you answer incorrectly.

GENERAL ADVICE

There are rules you can learn about the use of punctuation marks.

Do you know why the following punctuation marks are used?

- comma
- inverted commas
- colon
- semi-colon
- brackets (sometimes called parentheses)
- dashes
- capital letter

21. These sentences summarise what has happened in the passage by focusing on how the boys treat Tommy and how he reacts. For example, the boys have been 'cruel' as 'they always work him up like that' (1). This is effective as Tommy is the main character in the passage and his treatment by the boys is the main event (1).

EXPLANATION

You may be asked about the conclusion of a passage – this means how the passage ends. You may be referring to a word, a phrase, a sentence or a paragraph. Here you are asked about a short paragraph. Do you think it is an effective ending? If you look back over the passage, you will realise that what Ruth says here sums up what the passage has been about – Tommy's reaction when the boys treat him unkindly. The paragraph also focuses on Tommy who is the main character in the passage.

You will gain one mark for explaining whether you think the conclusion is effective and one mark for valid evidence that backs up your answer.

GENERAL ADVICE

Conclusions or endings:

- summarise the main ideas in a passage
- can provide the climax to a passage or provide dramatic effect (often using one word or phrase)
- link back to the beginning of a passage or to earlier idea(s) in the passage
- give an example or an illustration of a point(s) the writer has made earlier.

22. Kathy is protective towards Tommy/cares about Tommy/is concerned/worried about Tommy (1). 'He's going to be so sick if he ruins that shirt.' (1)

OR

Kathy thinks Tommy is stupid (1): 'if he's going to be that daft, he deserves what's coming.' (1)

OR

Kathy feels sorry for Tommy (1). She feels 'a little stab of pain' when she realises Tommy is not going to be picked (1).

EXPLANATION

Thinking about the whole passage, what is your opinion about how Kathy feels? What does she say and do about Tommy? Does she treat Tommy in the same way as other characters, such as Ruth? Does she approve or disapprove of the boys not picking Tommy?

You should know a lot of information about Kathy, having worked through all the previous questions. Use this to work out how she feels. Then look through to find a quote to back this up. Remember, you can choose words from anywhere in the passage.

GENERAL ADVICE

Read the last two questions carefully. They ask you about the whole passage. Questions about the whole passage are often evaluation questions – they ask you to judge the passage or to give your opinion about an aspect of the passage. You must always quote to back up your answer.

---

23. Kathy remembers the football game very accurately as she describes what happened at the game in detail (1). 'I can remember how the sun was glinting'/'I remember thinking . . .' (1).

OR

Kathy does not remember the football game very accurately as she shows some signs of uncertainty (1): 'the chances are that's how it was for me too'/'Or maybe I'm remembering it wrong'/'maybe I did feel a little stab of pain' (1).

EXPLANATION

The passage contains many details about the football game – the picking process, the children watching, what Tommy was wearing, and so on. So, in some ways, Kathy seems to be a reliable narrator – she remembers accurately, clearly and in detail. However, she states several times that she is unsure about what happened or that she may be wrong.

You are being asked for your opinion in this question so you can choose whether you think she is reliable or not.

GENERAL ADVICE

In fiction, an 'unreliable narrator' is a narrator who may or may not be telling the truth or who has a particular point of view which may be different from that of the other characters. In other words, we are reading about one character's version of events.

When you are reading a fiction passage and thinking about the narrator, ask yourself:

- Who is telling or narrating the story?
- Is the passage written in the first person ('I/me/my') or the third person ('he/she/it')?
- Do other characters have different views of events?

---

24. The writer dislikes boarding schools (1) as the passage is about children at boarding school treating a fellow pupil badly/cruelly (1).

OR

The writer dislikes boarding schools (1) as he has chosen this as the setting for his novel about the cruelty of children (1).

EXPLANATION

You will gain one mark for explaining the writer's attitude and one mark for evidence which backs this up. The pupils either ignore Tommy or treat him badly (even Kathy) so the writer is not creating a positive, pleasant description of boarding school.

GENERAL ADVICE

Remember that a writer always has an attitude to what he/she is writing whether the writing is fiction or non fiction. It is sometimes easier to spot a writer's attitude in non-fiction because the writer can explain directly what he or she thinks or feels. In fiction, the writer's attitude is conveyed through the characters or the setting or the theme or the writer's choice of words.

| PRACTICE EXAM E | CREDIT LEVEL WORKED ANSWERS |

1. Estha had never been talkative/never talked a lot (1) – he had 'always been a quiet child' (1).
   OR
   He had become silent gradually/over time (1). We are told 'there wasn't an exactly when'/'It had been a gradual winding down'/'a barely noticeable quietening' (1).

EXPLANATION

When you are asked to 'quote to support your answer' you should give the answer in your own words and then find evidence – actual words – from the passage to back up your answer. Look above at how the answer has one part in the candidate's own words and one part in quotation marks.

GENERAL ADVICE

Examiners use different ways to ask you to quote from the passage.

Look at the phrases below and get to know them – they are all asking you to quote!

- Quote from the passage
- Illustrate your answer from the passage (this does not mean draw a picture!)
- Refer closely to/by close reference to the passage
- Identify the word/phrase
- Write down the word/phrase
- What expression . . .?

2. Here the writer chooses to repeat the word 'never' three times (1). This repetition is effective as it emphasises how complete Estha's silence was (1).

EXPLANATION

In word choice questions, you should comment on:

- the specific words the writer has used/the technique(s) used

  and

- the effect of these words/techniques.

To gain full marks, quote the words – look at the first part of the answer where 'never' is quoted. Then explain the effect of the words – look at the second part of the answer above. Repetition is often used to emphasise a point or to make it stand out.

GENERAL ADVICE

You will always be asked to analyse the writer's craft at Credit level. In other words, you will be asked about the choices the writer has made about word choice, language and structure.

When you are asked about word choice, you should analyse the language the writer uses – why he/she has chosen particular words/phrases/images.

When answering, many pupils explain only what a word, phrase or sentence **means**. You should explain what it means **and** why it has been used/is effective to gain full marks.

3.   Inanimate means not living/lifeless (1). This word is placed immediately after a list of inanimate objects/the phrase 'blend into the background' tells me he is very still/the word 'invisible' tells me he is very still (1).

EXPLANATION

Always look at the words or phrases before a word as well as those which come after it to help you work out the meaning. Here the phrase 'blend into the background' and the list of inanimate objects 'bookshelves, gardens, curtains, doorways, streets' and the word 'invisible' all help you to work out the meaning. 'Inanimate' does not mean 'invisible' so you will gain no marks for this answer, unfortunately!

GENERAL ADVICE

What should you do if you don't know the meaning of a word? Here is the best way to work it out.

Context means the words and phrases round about the word or phrase itself. You should look at the context of the word because it may contain words or phrases which have a similar meaning or may help you work out the meaning of the word or phrase in question. Remember that the context refers to all the words and phrases just before and just after the word.

4.   Any two from:
     It took strangers a long time to notice Estha (1).
     AND/OR
     They did not realise that he did not speak (1).
     AND/OR
     They did not notice anything about him (1).

EXPLANATION

This is an understanding question – most candidates find these the easiest to answer as you are simply being asked to understand and explain ideas in the passage. Remember that highlighting or underlining key words or phrases in the question can help.

Here you could have highlighted 'strangers' and 'react'. The phrases 'quote to support' or 'answer in your own words' are NOT used here, so you can choose how to answer. You can quote from the passage or you can answer in your own words.

5.   This sentence summarises what we are told in the first two paragraphs about Estha being ignored or insignificant (2).

EXPLANATION

'What is the function of this sentence?' means 'What does this sentence **do**?'

In this case, the sentence **summarises** all we have learned about Estha in the previous two paragraphs. Did you notice how many marks are available here? For full marks, you have to explain that this sentence summarises the first two paragraphs. You will gain no marks if you only answer that the sentence summarises.

GENERAL ADVICE

You may be asked at Credit level to explain the function of a word, phrase or sentence. For example, you could be asked about the function of a sentence at the beginning or at the end of a paragraph (sometimes called a topic sentence) or the function of a single word.

The function of a word or phrase can be to:

- summarise
- explain
- show a result
- show a contrast
- give an example
- link with what has gone before or what comes after

There is sometimes a key word or phrase which 'signals' the function to you. However, there is sometimes no 'signal' word or phrase to help you work out the function – you have to work this out from the words of the sentence itself.

Look at the linking words and phrases below – can you work out their functions?

- in short
- furthermore
- the former ... the latter ...
- besides
- since
- as a result
- nonetheless
- unlike
- however

When you are asked about the function of a word or sentence or paragraph, you do not need to explain what the word or sentence(s) means.

6. The capital letter makes Estha's return seem an important or significant event (2).

EXPLANATION

Questions about capital letters are not too difficult – other than to begin a sentence or for the names of people and places, they are used to add importance to the meaning of the word.

Did you notice the allocation of marks is the same as for question 5? You get two marks for giving the correct answer and no marks if you answer incorrectly.

GENERAL ADVICE

You are likely to be asked at Credit level about punctuation – usually the question asks you about the function of a punctuation mark. This is one of the most straightforward questions to answer because there are rules you can learn about the use of punctuation marks!

Do you know why the following punctuation marks are used?

- commas
- inverted commas
- colons
- semi-colons
- brackets (sometimes called parentheses)
- dashes
- capital letters

7. He was not an outstanding/special/very clever/stupid student (1). He disliked working with others/spending time with others (1).

EXPLANATION

This is an understanding question (look back at question 2 for another example). Remember that highlighting or underlining key words or phrases in the question can help.

Here you could have highlighted 'type of student'. In the passage, there are several phrases which help you:

'not an exceptional student/backward/bad at anything'
'an average student'
'satisfactory work'
'does not participate in Group Activities'

All you have to do is explain these in your own words.

8. They were ashamed (1) at first (1).

EXPLANATION

You are being asked here to explain the phrase 'initial embarrassment'. Always look at the marks available to help you work out how many points to make/how much to write. Two marks mean you should make two points. If you answer 'ashamed' you will only gain one mark. You must also explain 'initial' in your own words.

The phrase 'explain fully' in the question also helps you to know you have to make more that one point!

---

9. Any two from:
He was quieter than their other customers (1).
AND/OR
They got to know him (1).
AND/OR
He never tried to lower the price of what he was buying (1).

EXPLANATION

The answers are all in paragraph 5 but you must answer in your own words – so once you have found the phrases 'grew to recognize him', 'amidst the clamoring of their other customers' and ' He never bargained', all you have to do is explain two of them in your own words.

---

10. (*a*) Estha is being compared to a 'bubble'. This image is effective (1) as it shows that Estha is enclosed/separate/still/removed from the noisy/turbulent/stormy world or 'sea of noise' around him (1).

(*b*) 'suddenly flooded in'/'A dam had burst'/'savage waters swept everything up in a swirling' (2).

EXPLANATION

When you are asked about effectiveness, you are being asked to evaluate how well the image works. You should also explain the image. So you are really being asked to do two things.

Look at the first part of the answer which explains that the image is comparing Estha to a bubble. Then the rest of the answer explains that this is an effective image because it conveys the idea that Estha is separate from what is happening around him.

You then have to look through paragraph 14. You know you are looking for an image to do with sea/water/bubbles – did you find all three images?

For part (a), you will gain one mark for saying whether the image is effective and one mark for a correct explanation of the image. For part (b), you will gain two full marks for a correct quote!

GENERAL ADVICE

At Credit level you will always be asked about imagery, which is a technique many fiction writers use. The three most common are:

* metaphor * simile * personification

You will sometimes be asked to identify which type of image is used. You may be given the image or you may have to find it for yourself. You then have to comment on how effective it is. A technique some pupils find helpful is to list as many similarities as possible between the object/movement/action/feeling itself and the object/movement/action/feeling to which it is compared. The more similarities, the more effective the image!

Remember that it is acceptable to explain that you do not find an image effective, but you must give good reasons for your answer.

11. Technique 1: *imagery/metaphor/personification* (1). 'enfolded him in its swampy arms'/'It rocked him'/'its stealthy, suckered tentacles'/'hoovering the knolls and dells'/'whisking them off the tip of his tongue'/'stripped his thoughts' (1).
Technique 2: *one word sentences* (1). 'Unspeakable'/'Numb' (1).

EXPLANATION

As you can see from the example answers here, you will gain one mark for identifying a technique and one mark for quoting correctly an example of this technique. The writer uses many images in this paragraph so there are plenty to choose from.

There are two different techniques here. You must identify both imagery **and** sentence structure to gain full marks for both parts of the question.

GENERAL ADVICE

You will always be asked to analyse the writer's craft at Credit level. In other words, you will be asked about the writer's word choice, language, structure.

When you are asked about structure, you should analyse the structure of phrases, sentences, paragraphs, the whole passage – why he/she has used particular or unusual patterns, order, organisation, e.g.

how the writer has chosen to punctuate the sentence
or
how long or short the sentence is and why
or
the pattern of the sentence and why it has been written in this way.

When answering, many pupils explain only what a word, phrase or sentence **means**. You should explain what it means **and** why it has been used/is effective to gain full marks. You have to comment on the effect of the punctuation, length or pattern; in other words, what the structure does and not just what it looks like!

12. 'entombed' means buried in a tomb/dead (1): 'hidden away . . . somewhere deep' shows that his silence is buried very deeply/permanently (1).

EXPLANATION

Always look at the words or phrases before a word as well as those which come after it to help you work out the meaning. Here the phrase 'hidden away' and 'somewhere deep' help you to work out the meaning.

GENERAL ADVICE

What should you do if you don't know the meaning of a word? Look at question 3 for advice about how to work it out from the context.

13. At first, Estha walks around the same area/only near where he lives/as though he is guarding something (1) but then he walks for longer distances/to other areas (1).

EXPLANATION

This is an understanding question about how Estha changes. Always look for key words or phrases which signal a change to the reader. The key phrase here is 'initially' which means 'at first' or 'to begin with'. The first part of the answer explains how Estha walked 'initially'; the second part of the answer explains how his walking changed – he 'went farther and farther afield'.

14. Any two from:
    'well-dressed' (1)
    'quiet walk' (1)
    'His face grew dark and outdoorsy.' (1)
    'Rugged.' (1)
    'Wrinkled by the sun.' (1)
    'With sea-secrets in him.' (1)

EXPLANATION

Remember that when you are asked for evidence from the passage, you can quote directly. You are looking for quotes which tell you that Estha looked wise. There are several to choose from in this paragraph.

15. The writer dislikes the idea of World Bank loans (1). This is shown by the writer using negative words such as 'smelled of shit and pesticides'/'Most of the fish had died'/'suffered from fin-rot'/ 'had broken out in boils' (1).

EXPLANATION

The writer's attitude or stance is conveyed by the words and ideas he chooses. Here, all the ideas are very negative; you are only asked for one reason but there are plenty to choose from.

You are asked to write down evidence from the passage meaning, you should quote one of these negative words or phrases directly. You will gain one mark for identifying the writer's attitude and one mark for valid evidence.

GENERAL ADVICE

Remember that a writer always has an attitude to what he/she is writing whether the writing is fiction or non-fiction. It is sometimes easier to spot a writer's attitude in non-fiction because the writer can explain directly what he or she thinks or feels. In fiction, the writer's attitude is conveyed through the characters or the setting or the theme or the writer's choice of words. You can work out the writer's attitude by thinking carefully about the words chosen and the associations these words have. These associations are called connotations which are suggested or implied meanings of a word. The literal meaning of a word is called its denotation.

16. The new houses are expensive/newly built/newly decorated/attractive (1).
    AND
    The old houses are less attractive/are hidden (1).

EXPLANATION

This is an understanding question – the new houses are described in the phrase 'new, freshly baked, iced, Gulf-money houses' which means they are newly built and attractive. The old houses are described as 'resentful' and 'green with envy' which means they are less attractive than the new houses. They are 'cowering' which means hiding. You will gain one mark for making a point about the new houses and one mark for a contrasting point about the old houses.

GENERAL ADVICE

Contrast questions are questions which ask you about the difference between two ideas/ characters/aspects. You must always make two points in your answer to a question about contrast because you are explaining the difference between **two** things.

17. The sentence contains a long list of (unconnected) items or ideas or feelings (1) which shows the number of different noises/the amount of commotion which Estha was suddenly able to hear and feel (1).

EXPLANATION

Questions about structure usually focus on the structure of sentences or paragraphs. You should look for unusual sentence structure, repetition, lists or patterns of words or phrases.

Did you spot that this is a list of unconnected concepts or things? You should identify the structure for one mark and comment on the effect of this structure for the second mark.

GENERAL ADVICE

Look back at question 11 for more advice on sentence structure.

18. It is a link because the phrase 'It had been quiet in Estha's head' refers back to the previous paragraphs which describe Estha's quietness (1). The second part of the sentence 'until Rahel came' introduces the change in Estha when Rahel arrives which is described in the following paragraphs (1).

EXPLANATION

If you are asked about a linking sentence, you should make two points – one about what has come before and one about what comes after the sentence. Answer the question by first quoting the words which link back – then explain what ideas they link back to. Then quote the words which look forward or introduce new ideas and explain these ideas. Look at the suggested answer above – can you spot the 'quote and explanation' in the first part of the answer and the 'quote and explanation' in the second part of the answer?

GENERAL ADVICE

A sentence (or word or paragraph) can have a linking function. Look back at question 5 for more advice on sentence function.

19. The phrase 'light and shade and light and shade' is an example of repetition (1). The use of repetition is effective as it mimics/reflects the pattern of light and shadow when travelling (1).

EXPLANATION

Here the use of repetition is identified then a reason given for why it has been used. You gain one mark for identifying that the writer has used repetition and one mark for your explanation.

20. 'Squelched' is an onomatopoeic word (1) which mimics/copies/reflects/sounds like the sound of wet mud (1).

EXPLANATION

Another analysis question which asks you about word choice; this time you are asked about onomatopoeia. You have to identify which onomatopoeic word is being used and, in addition, explain why this word is effective.

GENERAL ADVICE

What other onomatopoeic words do you know? Try saying them out loud to work out if they actually sound like the sound they are describing!

21. The mood or atmosphere is sad/depressing/miserable/gloomy (1).
    AND
    The paragraph describes Estha on his own/in the rain/lonely/wet/cold (1).

EXPLANATION

Remember that mood or atmosphere is always created through language. All the words and phrases below indicate that the mood or atmosphere is sad/depressing/miserable. Think about the meanings of these words and images – this is not a happy, light, playful scene!

'wetness'
'suddenshudder'
'rocked himself in the rain'
'wet mud'
'The cold puppy shivered'

GENERAL ADVICE

Mood (or atmosphere) means the feeling the writer creates. Writers create mood or atmosphere through the words and images they use. Some examples of mood are: playful, serious, sad, ironic, sarcastic, romantic ... Can you think of any more?

22. Estha was always a quiet child (1) so the description of him as silent is not a major change (1).
OR
As an adult, he began walking (1) and this seems to be a change for him (1).
OR
Estha changes when Rahel returns as he becomes very sensitive to noise and chaos (1) and he was not sensitive to this previously (1).

EXPLANATION

There are usually one or two questions at the end of the question paper which ask about the whole passage.

If you are asked about how a character develops or changes, think about the development or change as a series of steps. In this case, think about Estha as a child, as an adult and after Rahel returns.

Did you notice in the answer above that the candidate says that there was not a major change as Estha had always been quiet? You are being asked for your opinion so it is OK to agree or disagree – as long as you can justify your answer! You will gain one mark for explaining how Estha used to be/behave and one mark for saying what the change is

GENERAL ADVICE

The final questions in the Credit Close Reading Exam are usually evaluation questions – ones which ask for your opinion on an aspect of the passage. In your answer, you should:

- express your opinion
- explain your reasons for this in your own words
- refer to the text and/or quote from the text.

23. I do not feel sympathetic towards Estha (1) as we are not told the reason for his silence. His quietness is described in detail but there is no explanation given and he does not seem to be very likable because of this (1).
OR
I feel sympathy towards Estha (1) as he seems to be an unhappy character – we are told in detail about his quietness and I also think he is lonely as he is described as always walking on his own after his dog dies (1).

EXPLANATION

There are other reasons why you might sympathise with Estha which are not included here. The important thing to remember is that sympathy – or lack of it! – must be based on something the writer has conveyed to you about the character.

Did you spot the phrase in the question 'by referring closely to the passage'? This means you should give specific evidence – words, phrases, ideas – to back up your answer. You can use your own words (as in the first two suggested answers) or you can quote (as in the third suggested answer).

1.   They annoyed the neighbours by shining sunlight into their homes (1) with a broken piece of mirror (1).

EXPLANATION

You are told to use your own words so you cannot use 'reflecting' or 'shard'. You can see here that the candidate has used 'shining' instead of 'reflecting' and 'piece' instead of 'shard'.

Usually, the first question is not too difficult! Some pupils find it helpful to underline key words or phrases in the questions to help them focus on what is being looked for. In this question, the key phrase is 'annoy the neighbours'. So you know that you are looking for information about what the boys did that was annoying.

GENERAL ADVICE

Questions will usually follow the order of the passage. So, the first questions will usually ask you about the first few sentences or paragraphs of the passage. Then the questions will work through the passage chronologically (in the order that the events happened). Examiners write questions in this way to make things easier for you – so you will not have to jump around the passage to find the answers you are looking for!

---

2.   'a face like a Chinese doll' (1). This is effective as Hassan's face was round/he had a flat nose/he had narrow eyes/tiny ears/pointed chin like a doll's (1).
     OR
     'slanting, narrow eyes like bamboo leaves' (1). This is effective as his eyes are the same shape as bamboo leaves which are long and narrow (1).

EXPLANATION

First, find the simile! There are two to choose from. Did you spot them both?

When you are asked about effectiveness, you are being asked to evaluate how well the image works. You should also explain the image. So you are really being asked to do two things.

Look at the first part of the answer which quotes the simile. Then the rest of the answer explains that this is an effective image because it describes the shape/size of Hassan's face or eyes.

GENERAL ADVICE

At General level, you will always be asked about imagery which is a technique many fiction writers use – the three most common are:

*   metaphor
*   simile
*   personification

You will sometimes be asked to identify which type of image is used. You may be given the image or you may have to find it for yourself. You then have to comment on how effective it is. A technique some pupils find helpful is to list as many similarities as possible between the object/movement/action/feeling itself and the object/movement/action/feeling to which it is compared. The more similarities, the more effective the image!

Remember that it is acceptable to explain that you do not find an image effective, but you must give good reasons for your answer.

3. Hassan did everything the narrator asked (2).
    OR
    Hassan never refused to do what the narrator wanted (2).

EXPLANATION

Even if you were not sure of the meaning of 'denied', the sentence before this one – 'Hassan never wanted to, but if I asked, really asked, he wouldn't deny me.' – helps you as it shows that the narrator often asked Hassan to do things but we are told he 'never wanted to' do these things.

GENERAL ADVICE

Did you notice that you did not have to make two points in your answer this time – even though the question is worth two marks? Sometimes, examiners give two marks for the answer to a difficult question. If you do not give the correct answer you will be given 0 marks.

4. 'Deadly' (2)

EXPLANATION

Some pupils find it helpful to highlight words or phrases in the passage – either as they read through the passage for the first time or as they work through the questions. It's up to you. Highlighting can help you to find a word or phrase or idea. Here you could highlight the word 'deadly'.

Some pupils also find it useful to highlight words or phrases in the question. Here you could highlight 'good at using'. This can help you to focus on exactly what the question is asking you.

The highlighting technique can be very useful. Try it for yourself and see if it works for you.

5. He was 'as mad as someone as gentle as Ali could ever get' (1) which tells us that Ali was too calm/ kind/mild to be truly angry (1).
    OR
    We are told he would 'take the mirror' away or that he was 'scowling at his son' (1) which shows he was truly angry (1).

EXPLANATION

In this answer, you have to quote and then explain what the quote means – two suggestions are given here. These suggested answers place the quote first, then the explanation. The order is not important as long as you quote and explain.

You are being asked here to **find evidence from the passage**. This means you should quote words directly.

GENERAL ADVICE

There are different ways to ask you to quote from the passage. Look at the phrases below and get to know them – they are all asking you to quote!

*   Quote from the passage
*   Illustrate your answer from the passage (this does not mean draw a picture!)
*   Refer closely to/by close reference to the passage
*   Identify the word/phrase
*   Write down the word/phrase
*   What expression . . .?

6. well-off (2)

EXPLANATION

Always look at the words or phrases before a word as well as those which come after it to help you work out the meaning. Here the word 'affluent' is in the middle of a paragraph which describes in detail the very expensive house and its luxurious surroundings. So you could make a guess that affluent means well-off even if you did not know this word.

You will gain two full marks for getting this answer correct!

GENERAL ADVICE

What should you do if you don't know the meaning of a word? Here is the best way to work it out.

Context means the words and phrases round about the word or phrase itself. You should look at the context of the word because it may contain words or phrases which have a similar meaning or may help you work out the meaning of the word or phrase in question. Remember that the context refers to all the words and phrases just before and just after the word or phrase.

7. Any two from:
   'broad entryway' (1)
   'rosebushes' (1)
   'marble floors' (1)
   'wide windows' (1)
   'Intricate mosaic tiles' (1)
   'four bathrooms' (1)
   'Gold-stitched tapestries' (1)
   'crystal chandelier' (1)
   'vaulted ceiling' (1)

EXPLANATION

You are looking in paragraph 3 for examples of the prettiness of the house. You are not told to answer in your own words so you know you can quote directly from the passage. Did you highlight the phrase 'from the section after this phrase' so that you looked after the phrase and not earlier in the paragraph? Always read the question carefully!

8. Quotation marks are used to show that this is an alternative name/the name used by Baba/the narrator's name for Baba's study (2).

EXPLANATION

Writers use quotation marks for many different reasons. Did you realise that 'the smoking room' is also called the study? We are not told the reason why it is called 'the smoking room' so you can suggest a reason based on your knowledge of the passage.

GENERAL ADVICE

You should learn about the various punctuation marks and how and why they are used. You may be asked about:

- colons
- semi-colons
- dashes

- brackets
- commas
- exclamation marks

- question marks
- inverted commas
- quotation marks

Find out about the different uses of these punctuation marks. This will be useful in your own writing, too!

9. Any two from:
   laid back/relaxed (1)
   smoked pipes (1)
   talked (1)

EXPLANATION

Did you highlight the phrases 'Baba and his friends reclined on black leather chairs' or 'They stuffed their pipes' or 'discussed their favorite three topics'? You should choose any two of these and explain them in your own words.

10. *(a)* They are used to show that the phrase 'except Baba always called it "fattening the pipe"' is adding further information to the sentence (2).

    (b) 'neither one smiling – I am a baby'/'thirty guests – and, given my father's taste' (1).

EXPLANATION

Dashes are used to separate a phrase which adds more detail, information or further explanation.

Did you notice the allocation of marks for question 10(a) is the same as for question 3? You get two marks for giving the correct answer and no marks if you answer incorrectly.

---

11. Baba does not spend a lot of time with his son (1).
AND any **one** quote from:
'Go on, now' (1)
'This is grown-ups' time' (1)
'go and read one of those books' (1)
'close the door' (1)
'always grown-ups' time' (1)
'I sat there for an hour, sometimes two, listening to their laughter' (1)

EXPLANATION

You are being asked about the relationship between Baba and his son. There is plenty of evidence in this paragraph that Baba spends time with adults and not his son!

Look out for another question later about this relationship.

---

12. Built specially/to order/individually designed/built for a specific space/to a specific size (1).
The room had a curved wall so the cabinets had to be built to fit (1).

EXPLANATION

This is a difficult question so you gain two full marks for getting it correct! Did you highlight the phrase 'curved wall'?

GENERAL ADVICE

Look back at question 6 for more advice on working out meaning.

---

13. (i)   The narrator's grandfather and King Nadir Shah (1).
    (ii)   Baba and his wife/the narrator's mother (1).
    (iii)   Baba, Rahim Khan and the narrator as a baby (1).

EXPLANATION

Always read through the passage carefully. In this paragraph there is a lot of detail so highlighting phrases about photographs and the names of people might help you to work out who is in which photograph. The first photo is described after the phrase 'an old, grainy photo of ...' The second photo is described in the sentence beginning 'There was a picture of my parents' wedding night ...' The third is a little more difficult as the word 'Here' indicates there is a third photograph.

You will gain one mark for correctly identifying which people are in each of these three photographs.

---

14. The photograph of Baba and the narrator's mother is the best (1) because Baba is described as 'dashing' meaning handsome and his mother is smiling (1).

    OR

    The photograph of the narrator's grandfather is best (1) as it is exciting/it shows a dead deer/a hunting scene (1).

    OR

    The photograph of the narrator as a baby is best (1) because he has his fingers curled round Rahim Khan's finger and this demonstrates the bond between them (1).

EXPLANATION

Did you notice the phrase 'in your opinion' at the beginning of the question? It is up to you which photo you choose! The third photo shows Baba and Rahim Khan not smiling and tired so you might not choose this one. However, it also shows the closeness of Rahim Khan and the baby. As long as you give a sensible reason for your answer, you should gain two marks – one for choosing a photograph and one for giving a valid explanation of why you like it best.

15. (a) There was a large number of guests/at least 30 guests (1)

    AND/OR

    they happened often/regularly (1)

    AND/OR

    guests sat at an expensive wooden table (1).

    (b) 'modest' (2)

EXPLANATION

Did you know that 'extravagant' means spending an excessive amount of money? If not, could you work it out from what we are told about the parties – 'a mahogany table that could easily sit thirty guests' and 'almost every week'? 'Modest' means inexpensive, humble, small.

16. Ailing means sick or ill (1) and we are told the corn 'never really took' which means it did not grow well (1).

EXPLANATION

In this answer, it is important to explain the meaning of 'ailing' as well as explaining why it is appropriate. The number of marks helps you to work out that you have to do two things – give the meaning for one mark and explain why it is appropriate for one mark. Did you know that 'ailing' means sick or ill?

17. The paragraph tells us that the narrator's mother died giving birth to him which is important/shocking/surprising (1) and placing this sentence on its own emphasises this importance (1).

EXPLANATION

You are being asked here about the structure of this sentence – it is a paragraph on its own which consists of only one sentence. Did this sentence stand out to you when you read the passage? It is always a good idea to look out for unusual structures, for example, unusual sentence length. This is because examiners will ask you about unusual patterns and why they have been used!

GENERAL ADVICE

You are very likely to be asked about structure at General level. These are usually questions which ask you about unusual patterns in sentences or paragraphs.

In sentence structure questions, you should comment on:

how the writer has chosen to punctuate the sentence

or

how long or short the sentence is and why

or

the pattern of the sentence and why it has been written in this way.

In paragraph structure questions, you should comment on:

how long or short the paragraph is and why

or

the pattern of the paragraph and why it has been written in this way.

You can learn more about structure in Leckie and Leckie book, *Standard Grade English Course Notes*.

18. The narrator and Hassan led different lives (2).
OR
The narrator was rich and Hassan was poor (2).

EXPLANATION

You are asked for your opinion, so think about what you are told in paragraph 8 about the 'mansion' and the 'mud shack'. Perhaps the narrator felt uncomfortable in a less expensive and much smaller house! The difference in their homes tells you something about the relationship between the two boys – perhaps this is not a strong friendship.

19. Paragraph 9 repeats the information in paragraph 7 about where and when Hassan was born (1) and gives more detail about this event/more explanation/information about Hassan's mother (1).

EXPLANATION

'How does it link ...?' means 'what is the connection?' between these two paragraphs. How are they similar? They both mention the place and date of Hassan's birth – in fact, the first sentence of paragraph 9 is very similar to the first sentence of paragraph 7. Paragraph 9 goes on to give more information about Hassan's birth. There are two marks here so you must make these two points.

GENERAL ADVICE

There is sometimes a key word or phrase which 'signals' that the function of a word, sentence or paragraph is to link or connect ideas. (There is sometimes no 'signal' word or phrase to help you work out the function – in which case you have to work this out from the words of the sentence itself.)

Look at the linking words and phrases below.

- in short
- furthermore
- the former ... the latter ...

- as a result
- besides
- since

- nonetheless
- unlike
- however

20. (*a*) She died/she died from losing blood (2).

(*b*) She escaped/fled/took up with a group of musicians/entertainers (2).

EXPLANATION

The answer to question 20(a) is in the second sentence of paragraph 9 – did you know that 'haemorrhage' means bleeding? The answer to question 20(b) is in the third sentence of paragraph 9. We are told that Hassan 'lost' his mother and that she did something which was considered worse than death – she ran away.

You will gain two full marks for each correct answer!

---

21. Most Afghans would think this was very bad behaviour/a terrible thing to do/something which is shameful (2).

EXPLANATION

Did you know the meaning of the phrase 'a fate worse than death'? This phrase is sometimes used humorously but here it is used seriously.

Highlighting the phrase 'what most Afghans would think' in the question and highlighting the phrase 'most Afghans considered' in the passage might help you to find the answer which comes directly after these words.

GENERAL ADVICE

Always use any information you are given about the passage to help you. This is called the rubric – the one or two lines before you start reading the passage which tell you the name of the author, perhaps the title of the book and so on.

The information you are given here – that the passage is about 'a childhood friendship in Afghanistan' – tells you the setting of the extract. So you can work out, if you did not know it, that the word 'Afghan' might mean a person who comes from Afghanistan.

---

22. This is an effective opening (1) because the writer provides a lot of detail about the narrator and Hassan's relationship. For example, the writer describes the games they play together: 'Hassan and I used to climb the poplar trees in the driveway of my father's house and annoy the neighbours by reflecting sunlight into their homes with a shard of mirror.' (1)
OR
This is an effective opening (1) because it shows that the narrator seems to be more powerful than Hassan. For example, Hassan never complains about how the narrator treats him and it is obvious that their homes and lives are different: 'I went past the rosebushes to Baba's mansion, Hassan to the mud shack where he had been born, where he'd lived his entire life.' (1)

EXPLANATION

You will have thought about the openings of novels when working on literature as part of your Standard Grade English course. This should help when you are asked about openings in a Close Reading passage.

Of course, you could say that you do not think the opening is effective – as long as you can justify your answer with evidence from the passage.

GENERAL ADVICE

The answers given here are examples of how you might answer this question. As always with 'evaluation' questions, base your answer on the passage but include your own opinions. Remember that 'evaluate' means you are being asked to judge how well the writer has done something.

Whatever reasons you give, make sure you use quotes or evidence from the passage to back up your answer.

PRACTICE EXAM F   CREDIT LEVEL WORKED ANSWERS

1. On the grass outside the morgue/'on a patch of scrubby grass'/through the grid of an air vent (1).
   AND
   In the afternoon/one afternoon/late in the afternoon (1).

EXPLANATION

You will gain one mark for answering 'where' Lin Shui saw Alice and one mark for answering 'when' she saw Alice. Did you look in the right place for the answer which comes after 'But when Alice comes ...'? Did you spot the phrases 'one afternoon' and 'on a patch of scrubby grass'?

You are not asked to answer in your own words so you can choose to quote from the passage if you wish.

GENERAL ADVICE

Understanding questions ask you about ideas or information in the passage. This is one of the main types of question you will be asked. These questions are checking whether you have understood what the passage is all about.

To answer understanding questions, first work out what the question is asking. Then find the answer in the passage. These questions usually ask you to answer in your own words but not always – so be sure to check.

Many pupils find highlighting key words or phrases in the question and in the passage itself very helpful.

2. She is not interested (1): 'their heads are dull and ordinary' (1)/'they cannot sustain me' (1).
   She is interested (1): 'I watch' (1)/'I observe' (1)/'True, I am curious' (1).

EXPLANATION

This is another understanding question. You have a choice here. Did you notice that Lin Shui is both interested (she watches and observes the other children) and not interested (she knows they are not interesting or strong enough for her to take over)?

You are asked to quote to support your answer. Highlighting words and phrases in the passage is always helpful – look at the advice for question 1 above.

Remember to write down if Lin Shui is interested or not in the first part of your answer! Then quote in the second part of your answer.

GENERAL ADVICE

Questions usually follow the order of the passage. So, the first questions will usually ask you about the first few sentences or paragraphs of the passage. Then the questions will work through the passage chronologically (in the order that the events happened). Examiners write questions in this way to make things easier for you – so you will not have to jump around the passage to find the answers you are looking for! Usually, the question will tell you where to look for example, 'Read paragraph 1 again' or 'in the first paragraph'.

3. Any two from: Alice's appearance/size/complexion/hair/eyes/calmness (1) for two marks.

EXPLANATION

Did you know that 'spellbound' means fascinated, mesmerised, entranced? Look at these quotes from the passage which all appear after the sentence 'But when Alice comes I am spellbound' – 'a slip of a thing' (her size), 'pale'(her skin/complexion), 'her long hair always moving' (her hair), 'moons of contemplation' (her eyes).

You could also explain that Lin Shui is fascinated because Alice seems so calm – 'it does not seem to worry her' – as you are asked to give two different reasons.

There is one mark for each reason.

4. This is an effective image as it compares Alice's skin/colour/complexion (1) to the colour of the froth/foam of a wave (1).

EXPLANATION

When you are asked about effectiveness, you are being asked to evaluate how well the image works. You should also explain the image. So you are being asked to do two things.

Look at the first part of the answer which explains that the image is referring to Alice's skin or complexion. Then the rest of the answer explains that this is an effective image because it describes the colour of Alice's skin, which is the same colour as the froth or foam on a wave. You will gain no marks for saying Alice's skin is the colour of cream – you must include in your answer the idea of the froth or foam on a wave.

GENERAL ADVICE

At Credit level, you will always be asked about imagery which is a technique many fiction writers use – the three most common are:

- metaphor
- simile
- personification

You will sometimes be asked to identify which type of image is used. You may be given the image or you may have to find it for yourself. You then have to comment on how effective it is. A technique some pupils find helpful is to list as many similarities as possible between the object/movement/action/feeling itself and the object/movement/action/feeling to which it is compared. The more similarities, the more effective the image!

Remember that it is acceptable to explain that you do not find an image effective .... but you must give good reasons for your answer.

---

5. The entrance is empty/gaping open/wide open/shaped like an open mouth (1) which makes the entrance or doorway seem frightening or ominous (1).

EXPLANATION

In word choice questions, you should comment on the specific words the writer has used

AND

the effect of these words.

Here you should think about the words 'yawning' and 'mouth' and what these tell you about the entrance – if something is gaping open then it may look frighteningly empty. Explain the meaning of 'yawning mouth' for one mark and explain the effect for the second mark.

GENERAL ADVICE

This is an 'analysis' question. You will always be asked to analyse the writer's craft at Credit level. In other words, you will be asked about the choices the writer has made about structure and language. You could be asked to analyse the effect of:

how the writer has organised the passage

OR

the style of language the writer uses

OR

the structure of phrases, sentences, paragraphs.

When answering, many pupils only explain what a word, phrase or sentence **means**. You should explain what it means **and** comment on the structure or word choice **and** why it has been used/is effective to gain full marks.

6. Any two from:

'shoulders open the . . . door' (1)

'rusty-hinged' (1)

'It shudders' (1)

It 'grumbles' (1)

It 'sticks a bit' (1)

EXPLANATION

The key phrase here is 'shoulders open the rusty-hinged door' – did you highlight it? You could choose to look for the answer **before** the word 'door' for example, 'rusty-hinged' meaning it would be difficult to open. Or you could look for the answer **after** the word 'door' for example, 'sticks a bit'.

GENERAL ADVICE

Examiners use different ways to ask you to quote from the passage. The word 'evidence' is often used. This is just another way of asking you to quote. Look at the phrases below and get to know them – they are all asking you to quote!

1. Support your answer with evidence
2. Quote from the passage
3. Which word/phrase…?
4. Use/find/give evidence
5. Give an example
6. Illustrate your answer (this does not mean draw a picture!)
7. Refer closely to the passage
8. Identify the word(s)
9. Write down the word(s)
10. What expression …?

---

7. It is dark/dirty/old/cold/damp/mysterious/empty/sad/depressing/miserable (1).

AND

'gloom'/'stale, dead air'/'stains on floor'/'paint is flaking'/'echoes of the past' (1).

EXPLANATION

You are asked about the inside of the morgue. So you should look for the answer in the passage after Alice has entered the morgue – from 'She takes a few steps' onwards.

Remember that mood or atmosphere is always created through language. All of the quotes above indicate that the mood or atmosphere is sad/depressing/miserable. Think about the meanings of these words and images – this is not a happy, light, playful scene!

GENERAL ADVICE

Analysis questions include questions about how the author creates mood (or atmosphere) – the feeling the writer creates. Writers create mood or atmosphere through the words and images they use. Some examples of mood are: playful, serious, sad, ironic, sarcastic, romantic ... Can you think of any more?

8. The author's word choice is effective because 'scum' means a worthless person (1) so Lin Shui is suggesting she is unwelcome or has no value (1).
   OR
   The writer's word choice is effective because 'scum' means a dirty or impure film on the top of a liquid (1) so Lin Shui is suggesting she is dirty, impure or unwanted (1).

EXPLANATION

In word choice questions, you should comment on the specific words the writer has used **and** the effect of these words. When you are asked about effectiveness, you are being asked to evaluate how well the word works.

Look at the first part of the answer which explains the meaning of the word 'scum'. 'Scum' has two meanings – perhaps you only knew one meaning or you knew both meanings. If you knew both, choose the one that you are most comfortable explaining. Then, in the second part of the answer, explain the effect of choosing this word – the author has chosen this word because it conveys the idea of something negative, worthless or unwanted.

You will gain one mark for explaining why you think the writer's word choice is effective and one mark for a valid explanation of what this suggests.

GENERAL ADVICE

Look back at question 5 for advice on word choice questions.

9. Repetition of the phrase 'her every ...'/the use of the words 'heartbeat', 'thought', 'memory'. 'experience', 'emotion'/emphasise(s) how fully Lin Shui inhabits Alice / how Lin Shui takes over every aspect of Alice (1).

EXPLANATION

There are two marks here – you are given one mark for identifying the repetition or particular words the writer uses and one mark for explaining what the effect of this technique is.

Did you spot the repetition of 'her every ...'? If a word is repeated, its meaning is emphasised.

10. Any three from:
    'at last'/'dawdle'/'wait'/'haul us up'/'stroll'/'up a long road'/'past a shop called the Dairy Farm, then along a path' for two marks.

EXPLANATION

There are plenty of words and phrases to choose from here. You could pick any word or phrase which tells you that the journey was slow or that they took their time or that it was a long way.

Read the question carefully – the phrase 'from the beginning of the paragraph' means you should choose answers from the first 2 or 3 lines only.

GENERAL ADVICE

Sometimes it is tricky to work out how marks are allocated! You are sometimes asked for three pieces of evidence for two marks. It works like this:

three pieces of evidence = 2 marks

two pieces of evidence = 1 mark

one piece of evidence = no marks.

11. She was murdered twenty five years previously and the area may have changed (2).

OR

She may never have visited The Peak before (2).

OR

She may never have taken over another person before (2).

OR

The Peak is an exclusive, wealthy district and Lin Shui may be poor (2).

OR

Few Chinese people live on The Peak (2).

EXPLANATION

You are asked for your opinion here so you can use your own general knowledge to help you answer the question. Did you notice that you are told in the introduction to the passage that Lin Shui is Chinese and was murdered 25 years previously? This is why you should always read the introduction!

There is plenty of evidence in the passage to help you, too. There is information about the Peak Tram, the roads and general area, the people living on The Peak and so on.

You are asked for your opinion, which means there is no wrong answer as long as you write something that is based on your knowledge of the passage and your own common sense.

GENERAL ADVICE

Questions that ask for your opinion can be called 'evaluation' questions. In other words, you are being asked to make a judgement about what you are reading.

You may be asked to back up your opinion with reasons – usually called 'evidence'. Remember that when you see the word 'evidence' in a Close Reading question you should write down words or phrases from the passage.

12. Any two from:

Alice has two parents whereas Lin Shui only had her father (1).

AND/OR

Alice's father is often away whereas Lin Shui looked after her father (1).

AND/OR

Alice has a mother but Lin Shui had no mother (1).

EXPLANATION

Read the question carefully. This question refers to paragraph 3. All the information about the parents of the girls in paragraph 3 appears between the phrases 'When I was alive ...' and '... educated in England'. Remember not to include information from paragraph 4.

GENERAL ADVICE

Remember that questions follow the order of the passage. Highlighting key words and phrases in the question often helps you to look for the answer in the right place.

13. She finds it surprising (1): 'seems strange' (1).

OR

She finds it surprising that Alice is lonely (1) as there are 'so many people about' (1).

OR

She thinks it is 'lucky' (1) as it means Alice will like being possessed by her (1).

EXPLANATION

The section to look at is 'It seems strange to me that, with so many people about, Alice should be lonely. But she is. I feel it. Still, it is lucky, because it means that she will probably welcome my company.'

Did you notice that there are two possible answers here – Lin Shui thinks Alice being lonely is strange and lucky. So you can choose which answer to give. You will gain one mark for correctly explaining how Lin Shui feels and one mark for an appropriate quote.

14. It is empty (1).
AND/OR
There are few people in the flat (1).
AND/OR
Alice's parents are away or distant (1).

EXPLANATION

There are two marks available for this question. This means you should make two points in your answer. You should explain that the flat is empty AND make another point for the full two marks.

GENERAL ADVICE

Always check how many marks are available for a question. This gives you an indication about how much to write. Also, you are given space on the question paper to write your answer. The amount of space given is also a guide to how much to write. If there are three lines, you are expected to write more than a few words!

---

15. This sentence mentions Alice's sisters ('they') and the remainder of the passage is about one of the sisters, Jillian (2).
OR
This sentence indicates that Alice's family is not what Lin Shui expected and the next section gives an example of this. (Jillian and Alice's behaviour in the kitchen.) (2)

EXPLANATION

You may be asked about the function of a sentence, phrase, word or idea. Here you are asked about a sentence. The function of a sentence means what it is for – not what does it mean!

The key words here are 'when they return home' and 'is not as I imagined it'. As you have already read the whole passage, you know that the rest of the extract describes Jillian eating in the kitchen. So this is a linking sentence that introduces a new subject – one of Alice's sisters. You could also explain that the next part of the passage gives an example of an incident which is not what Lin Shui had imagined.

You will gain two full marks for a correct answer!

GENERAL ADVICE

A sentence may contain a word or phrase that refers back to a previous idea or forward to a new idea. This is called 'linking'.

Authors sometimes use 'linking words' which make this easier to spot! Look out for linking words and phrases such as:

- in short
- furthermore
- the former ... the latter ...

- besides
- since
- as a result

- nonetheless
- unlike

---

16. The description is effective as it contains lists of types of food (1) that emphasise how much/the variety/the amount of food Jillian was eating (1).
OR
The description is effective as the word 'stuffing'/slathered'/'cramming' (1) emphasises how much food Jillian was eating/that Jillian was overeating (1).

EXPLANATION

Did you focus on sentence structure in your answer – the list of foods, for example, 'biscuits and cakes and crisps and chocolate' or did you focus on word choice, for example, 'cramming'?

You can choose to answer either on sentence structure or word choice as long as you explain the effect of this.

GENERAL ADVICE

When you write about structure, you should analyse the structure of phrases, sentences, paragraphs, the whole passage – why has he/she used particular or unusual patterns, order, organisation? You might look at

how the writer has chosen to punctuate the sentence

OR

how long or short the sentence is and why

OR

the pattern of the sentence and why it has been written in this way.

When answering, many pupils explain only what a word, phrase or sentence means. You should explain what it means and why it has been used/is effective to gain full marks. You have to comment on the effect of the punctuation, length or pattern; in other words, what the structure does and not just what it looks like!

17. She makes one of the kitchen lights flash on and off (1) for fun: 'I amuse myself'/'I think it is very funny' (1).

EXPLANATION

You will find the answer after the phrase 'as if infused with life force'. You are given one mark for 'how' she reacts and one mark for 'why' she reacts by making the light flash. Did you highlight the words 'how' and 'why' in the questions?

When you are asked to 'quote to support your answer' you should give the answer in your own words and then find evidence – actual words – from the passage to back up your answer.

18. This simile is effective as it compares Jillian to a puppet (1).
    AND
    This suggests she is being controlled by someone/she is moving in an uncontrolled way/she is out of control (1).

EXPLANATION

Did you work out that Jillian looks like a jerking puppet because of the flashing tube light? So the simile tells you something about how she is moving. Did you also realise that Jillian's eating and drinking is out of control? A puppet's strings are controlled by a puppeteer so the puppet itself has no control. This is a very effective simile! You will gain one mark for explaining the comparison between Jillian and a puppet and one mark for explaining why you find it effective.

GENERAL ADVICE

Look at question 4 for more advice on imagery.

19. She is serious/she watches with no expression on her face/she does not find it funny (1): 'po-faced' (1).

EXPLANATION

The answer is in the last sentence of the paragraph. Did you know that 'po-faced' comes from the phrase 'poker faced' meaning showing no expression or keeping a straight face?

You are given one mark for explaining how Alice reacts and one mark for a correct quote.

GENERAL ADVICE

What should you do if you don't know the meaning of a word? Here is the best way to work it out ...

Context means the words and phrases round about the word or phrase itself. You should look at the context of the word because it may contain words or phrases which have a similar meaning or may help you work out the meaning of the word or phrase. Remember that the context refers to all the words and phrases just before and just after the word.

20. (a) Technique: *word choice* (1). '[S]cuttle' means the cockroaches run quickly (1) **or** 'feast' means the cockroaches eat a large amount (1) **or** 'scrabble' means the cockroaches scratch or scrape as they move (1) **or** 'lumbers' means the cockroaches moved clumsily (1) **or** 'gobble' means the cockroaches gulp or eat hungrily (1).

OR

Technique: *onomatopoeia* (1). '[W]hirr' means the cockroaches fly with a humming or buzzing sound (1).

(b) Technique: *metaphor* (1). The cockroaches are 'the size of Hong-Kong dollars' which suggests they are large/round (1).

OR

Technique: *simile* (1). The cockroaches are 'as shiny as vinyl' which suggests they are smooth and polished (1).

OR

Technique: *alliteration* (1). The cockroaches are 'beetle-brown' which suggests they are the same colour as beetles (1) **or** the cockroaches 'gleam in the glow' which suggests they shine/ are lit up/reflect light (1).

EXPLANATION

When there are two parts to a question, always read <u>both</u> parts before you write your answer! The first part asks you about the cockroaches' behaviour and the second part asks about the cockroaches' appearance. First, think about which words/phrases in the passage refer to behaviour and which words/phrases in the passage refer to appearance. Then identify the techniques. Remember to identify the technique for one mark and then explain it for the second mark.

GENERAL ADVICE

At Credit level, you may be asked about any aspect of a writer's word choice including onomatopoeia and alliteration. You should be familiar with these techniques and practise spotting them. You should also practise explaining why an author has used a particular technique. For example, alliteration emphasises the words which are alliterated and draws attention to the sounds of the words – this is why it is often used in poetry.

---

21. She is unconcerned or she does not care (1).

AND

She stops eating 'just long enough' to kill it/she 'glances cursorily' at her hand which means a quick look/she 'starts guzzling again' immediately (1).

EXPLANATION

This is an understanding question which asks you about how Jillian feels. Look at how the writer describes what she does when she sees the cockroach. Then think about what her behaviour tells you about how she is feeling. That she is unconcerned is the first part of the answer for one mark. Quote one piece of evidence for the second mark.

---

22. Any two from:

Alice is lonely (1)

AND/OR

vulnerable (1)

AND/OR

has a distant/difficult/dysfunctional family (1)

AND/OR

is living in foreign country (1).

EXPLANATION

The key phrase in this question is 'why do you think'? You are being asked for your opinion. You should think about all you have learned about Alice in the passage to reflect on why she might welcome Lin Shui. You gain one mark for each reason.

GENERAL ADVICE

The final questions in the Credit Close Reading are usually evaluation questions – ones which ask for your opinion on an aspect of the passage. In your answer, you should:

express your opinion

AND

explain your reasons for this in your own words (If you are asked to do so).

You may be asked to quote or give evidence from the passage – as in question 24.

23. The writer wants to give Lin Shui's point of view (2).
OR
To show that Alice is silent/frustrated/has been taken over/has no voice (2).
OR
To show that Lin Shui becomes Alice's voice (2).

EXPLANATION

You are being asked for your opinion in this question so you can choose any of the reasons above.

You should be aware that writers choose whether to write in the first or third person – usually because they want to build up one character's view of the world.

You will gain two full marks for a correct answer!

GENERAL ADVICE

In fiction, a narrator has a particular point of view which may differ from that of the other characters. In other words, we are reading about one character's version of events.

When you are reading a fiction passage and thinking about the narrator, ask yourself:

* who is telling or narrating the story and why?

* is the passage written in the first person ('I/me/my') or the third person ('he/she/it')?

* do other characters have different views of events?

24. Lin Shui is hiding at the beginning of the passage/is watching other children secretly: 'I observe them' (2).
OR
Lin Shui secretly takes over Alice: 'I slide into her' (2).
OR
Jillian is over-eating secretly in the kitchen: 'starts guzzling again' (2).
OR
Lin Shui is a ghost and therefore a secretive or hidden character (2).
OR
Lin Shui makes things happen as she is hidden: 'causing one of the tube lights in the kitchen to flash' (2).
OR
Alice's mother 'feels far away' suggesting she is hiding something or is distant/secretive (2).

EXPLANATION

As you can see, there are plenty of examples from the passage of secrets or secretive behaviour. Always back up your opinion with evidence from the passage. You can quote or refer to ideas in the passage.

INTRODUCTION

This section gives you advice about the Standard Grade English Writing exam. The first part gives you general help with how to write in the exam. The second part looks at the questions themselves and gives you specific advice about how to tackle them.

As well as advice, you will find:

TOP TIPS

These are 'at a glance' tasks to do or advice to remember.

CREDIT CRUNCHES

These contain specific advice for pupils hoping to gain a Credit award.

All pupils – whether working at Credit, General or Foundation level – sit the same Writing paper. The Writing paper is in booklet form and contains anything between 20 and 25 questions/essay titles. There are also pictures and photographs on the left-hand side pages of the booklet. In the exam, you will choose **one** of the questions/essay titles.

You are given 75 minutes for this exam. You should always spend some of this time planning what you are going to write. Take your time at this stage – it is better to spend 10 minutes calmly choosing and planning your writing than to start writing in a hurry, change your mind and have to start all over again!

Give yourself an hour for the actual writing itself – how many words can you write in an hour? If you do not know, you should find this out. We all write at different speeds so you can only find this out on your own. Your friends could be very fast or very slow writers so don't compare yourself with them. Work out how much you can write and aim to be able to do this in the exam itself.

If you often run out of time, practice will help. For example, you may be trying to write stories which are simply too long – perhaps because you do not spend time on planning the plot/storyline and so try to cover too much in the story itself. Practise planning and writing simpler, shorter stories – fewer characters or fewer events perhaps – and this may help you to finish on time.

Always leave 5 minutes at the end for a final read through. Even if you have not finished your writing, try to take time for a check. Spelling and punctuation errors can spoil the overall effect of a piece of writing so take the time to ensure your sentences make sense.

TOP TIP

Every year, a number of pupils do not follow the instructions at the beginning of the paper which tell you to choose **one** question from the paper.

There are usually between 20 and 25 questions to choose from. Choose **one** only!

Preparation before the big day!

Lots of people will tell you that you can't prepare for the English Writing paper. The truth is that you **can** prepare for the Writing paper and the more preparation you do, the better your writing will be.

The best preparation is to write, write, write! Whether it is letters to your pen pal, stories, your diary or writing for other subjects like History, all writing practice will be useful when it comes to the exam. Of course, you will not know exactly what writing questions will be in the exam paper but you can practise by looking at past papers – or working through some examples from the Writing Paper in this book – because the same types of writing almost always appear in the paper. For example, there are usually questions which ask you to write short stories, to write about personal experience, descriptive writing and so on. So looking at past or practice papers will give you a very good idea of what to expect.

TOP TIP

The proper term for a type of writing is 'genre'. How many genres are there in English? Challenge yourself to see how many you can come up with!

Using pictures/photographs

Another good way to prepare for the exam is to look at photographs or pictures and use these pictures to help your writing. There are always pictures and/or photos in the Writing exam paper so this will be good practice for the exam day itself.

Don't just ignore the pictures in the paper (as many pupils do!). A photo or picture is there to help you. It can give you ideas and inspiration. Look at the picture in detail and think of words and ideas as you examine it. For example, you might be shown a photo of a dark, gloomy forest and one of the tasks is to write an atmospheric piece of descriptive writing. As you look closely at the picture, you may think of words like 'frightening', 'secretive' or 'silent'. You may even see a dim ruined castle in a corner of the picture and this might spark off an idea – perhaps you could include a description of the castle as well as the forest? Let your imagination run wild...

Don't worry if you find it challenging to use pictures for inspiration – you do not have to use ideas from the photo or picture at all if you do not want to. And there are always questions at the end of the paper without any pictures!

Choosing a genre

Another good idea is to practise more than one type of writing. You may love writing short stories and so you may have decided that is what you will write in the exam. But what if the short story questions in the exam do not appeal to you? Practise writing at least TWO genres to prepare for the exam. For example, you may enjoy writing informative pieces like news articles or reports but you could also practise your personal writing so you have more questions to choose from in the exam.

TOP TIP

Don't forget about spelling, punctuation and paragraphing. A good way to work on these aspects is to get someone – a teacher, a friend, your parent/carer – to look over your work. Get into the habit of reading over your work by reading it aloud in your head or to friends or family to make sure your writing makes sense.

On examination day

Firstly, punctuation, spelling and grammar. These are sometimes called the 'technical' aspects of English. All your sentences must make sense clearly 'at first reading'. This means the examiner should not have to re-read a sentence because the meaning is unclear. Place commas in the right places, especially when you are writing complex sentences. Do try to write as accurately as you can. Checking over your work by reading it to yourself can help to ensure your sentences make sense. If it doesn't make sense to you, it won't make sense to the examiner!

CREDIT CRUNCH

At General level, there might be a few errors in punctuation, spelling or grammar. So if you want to achieve Credit, try to eliminate these. Your sentence structure has to be accurate so practise writing long complex sentences with plenty of clauses. Read quality newspapers to find examples of interesting sentence structures.

For a Grade 1, your paragraphs and sentences have to be 'skilful'!

Now, length. Pupils often ask how long an essay written in an exam has to be. The simple answer is that there is no limit because we all write at different speeds and we all write different amounts. Also, think about your purpose. You might choose to write 'in any way' about a given title and choose to write a poem. A poem of, say, 600–700 words would be very long indeed! This is what is meant by the phrase 'appropriate to purpose'. The length should 'fit' the purpose and, of course, will be related to the amount of time you have in the exam.

Let's think some more about this idea of purpose. You must be very clear about the purpose of the writing task you choose. For example, you might choose to write a short story. One of the main purposes of a short story is to entertain the reader. So your story has to be entertaining! If your purpose is to create a gently humorous story which will make the reader laugh, then it must communicate this gentle humour. Otherwise, it won't 'fulfil its purpose'. Never change purpose in the middle of a piece of writing – if you start writing a short story about a character in a dilemma, don't get carried away so much that this turns into a personal story about a time when **you** were in a dilemma! You can, of course, think about your own experience and even use some of these details, but you must stick to the purpose in the question.

Words, words, words ...

What about the actual words you use? When writing, pupils can sometimes be so busy with character, setting, ideas, organisation, and all the rest that they forget about the actual words they are using! Try to use language in interesting and original ways – not just as words to tell a story or explain an experience or express an opinion.

You could use:

- imagery such as similes and metaphors
- interesting sentence structures – different sentence lengths and patterns
- language to create a mood or atmosphere, for example, to build up tension in a ghost story.

Have a look at the Practice Close Reading passages. The writers of these passages have all used interesting and original language!

CREDIT CRUNCH

For a Credit award, you have to use accurate vocabulary and you have to use a variety of words. Extend your vocabulary by reading as much as you can – and keep a dictionary beside you so that, when you come across a word you don't know, you can look it up and store it away for your own use. Reading quality newspapers will also help.

PERSONAL WRITING

1. Write about a memorable holiday. Remember to include your thoughts and feelings as well as describing your holiday experiences.
5. Are your schooldays the 'happiest days of your life'? Write about your experience of school. Remember to include your thoughts and feelings.
10. Write about how you make a contribution to helping others in this country or in the developing world.
13. Describe a memorable family occasion. Remember to include your thoughts and feelings.
21. As a teenager I was so insecure. I was convinced I had absolutely no talent at all.' (Johnny Depp)

   Write about an experience you have had where you overcame your insecurity or demonstrated a talent.

These questions are all examples of Personal Writing. The important thing to remember, whether you are writing about something that has already happened (for example, question 1) or about things which are happening now (for example, question 10), is to write 'from the heart'. The best Personal Writing is truthful and open and describes your feelings and emotions clearly. For example, if you do not remember a holiday particularly well, it would be difficult to pretend you remember every detail and to write honestly about how it made you feel.

Remember also that Personal Writing should include description of sights, sounds, surroundings, atmosphere – if you do not include this kind of description, your writing will end up being a list of events and nothing else. Try to make your writing lively and not just 'Then we did this', or 'Then I did that'! This is one reason why the question usually reminds you to include your thoughts and feelings.

> *Can you spot the differences between the two extracts below?*
>
> *We got up at 5 o'clock in the morning. We were very tired. We packed our cases and waited for the taxi. The taxi arrived and we went to the airport.*
>
> *We got up at 5 o'clock in the morning and looked out of the frosty, icy window. We were very tired but so excited to be heading off towards heat and sunshine! We packed our cases, the two of us sitting on them to make sure they closed. They sprang open every time we tried to stuff in another last minute 'essential'. At 6 o'clock the taxi arrived with a welcome honk of its horn and whisked us off to the airport.*

So this type of writing is about your emotions. It is about reflecting on how you felt or feel about something or someone. When you are writing about an experience, you should explain how you felt before, during and after the experience. For example, if you choose question 21, you might describe your feelings/emotions about your part in a school dance show:

- before the event (how you prepared for the dance show, for example, rehearsals)
- at the time of/during the event (describe the dance show itself)
- afterwards (how you felt after the show had ended).

This is called 'chronological order' – in other words, write about the events you are describing in the order that they happened. So, if you choose question 5 about your time at school, you could use the chronological order below:

- my first day at primary school
- my teacher and class
- first few years – great happy times, loved learning
- primary 5/6 – moved house and school, hated new school, loneliness
- secondary school – a 'fresh start', new friends, love new subjects
- how I feel now I am in S4.

In question 10, you will have to think about how you want to organise your writing. Perhaps you could think about the different ways you help others – your job at a nursing home, your involvement in charity fund raising, your plans for a gap year helping in an orphanage. So your writing would have three main sections.

Some pupils find mind maps helpful to organise their writing. Here is a mind map of the ideas for question 10 above.

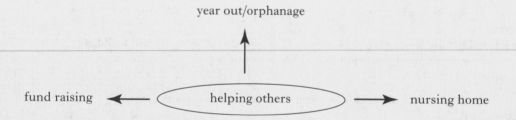

Remember that you can organise your Personal Writing in any way that 'fits' with what you are writing about – as long as it is organised!

Personal Writing is a very popular choice for many pupils. It is a chance to write about yourself and about something that has happened to you so, since everyone is different, no one will be able to write exactly the same as you. A lot of pupils choose this option so try to make your writing stand out. If you follow the advice above, you will be well on the way to writing success.

CREDIT CRUNCH

For a Credit award, you have to show 'insight and self-awareness' in your personal writing – so write about an experience that you have reflected on in depth and that has helped you learn things about yourself. You also have to express your feelings and reactions with 'sensitivity'. This means being able to understand and explain your emotions, showing you are aware of why you have acted or reacted in a certain way.

SHORT STORIES

2. Write a short story about someone on the holiday of a lifetime. You should develop setting, character and plot.

6. Write a short story using the following title: 'The School Bully'. You should develop setting, character and plot.

9. Write a short story using the following opening:
   'The children slipped as they climbed to the top, shouting to the little ones to hurry up and clawing at the stinking rubbish …'

14. Write a short story about uninvited guests at a party. You should develop setting, character and plot.

20. Write a short story in which the main character makes a mistake. You should develop setting and character as well as plot.

Usually, a short story question will help you with what you need to do – you will be told 'You should develop setting and character as well as plot.' So that is exactly what you should do!

Many pupils write short stories which have lots of action happening (the plot or storyline) but they forget to develop the setting of the story or the character(s).

Setting

TOP TIP

Describe the setting – both time and place. This can be done in chunks, for example, in a paragraph(s) near the beginning of your writing and/or can be spread throughout your writing.

Here is an example of description of setting (place) from the beginning of a story.

> The birthday cake lay trampled on the kitchen floor, candles and tiny bits of icing and sugar scattered over the table. The kitchen was ruined, chairs upset and cutlery, plates, cups all dirty and torn. Missy stood in the centre of the room, sobbing quietly.

Here is an example of description of setting (time) from the beginning of a story.

> It was the end of the war. Richard sighed as took off his khaki army uniform with its tight jacket and brass buttons and counted out his few remaining shillings. Time to go home.

Can you spot 'clues' to where and when these stories take place?

Characters

One very common mistake pupils make is to assume that the reader knows all about a character. But the reader can only know what you tell them! Remember that although you may feel you know a character, you need to describe him or her to the reader using plenty of detail.

So make sure you develop your character(s) – ask yourself:

- How does he/she change, develop, grow?
- How does he/she behave and speak?
- What does he/she look like?
- How does he/she relate to other people?
- What are his/her opinions/points of view?

Show what characters are like through the way they speak, act and through their relationships.

Theme

What will the theme of your story be? Sometimes, the question will tell you this – for example, in question 20, you are told that a character making a mistake will be the theme of the story – but how will you develop this theme? Will the mistake be life-threatening? What are the results of the mistake? How will the story end? Will your story have a moral or message?

TOP TIP

Popular themes include:

- relationships
- good versus evil
- freedom
- conflict
- love

Can you think of any others you would like to write about?

CREDIT CRUNCH

For a Grade 1 or 2, you should show you are skilled in all the aspects of fiction writing above – creating and developing character, describing setting, exploring theme... and it goes without saying that examiners are looking for great imagination in Credit short story writing!

Whatever grade you are aiming to achieve, you will have to organise your story. It goes without saying that it needs to have a beginning, a middle and an end. Usually, a story will build towards a climax near the end. For example, if you are answering question 20, the mistake could happen about two-thirds of the way through the story – after you have built up your plot and developed your characters. After your character makes the mistake, you could write about the effects of this.

You can use techniques such as flashback to create a more interesting structure. The important thing is to plan out the structure before you start. That way, your story won't ramble and the reader will be able to follow the plot clearly.

Short stories are also very popular with pupils – so try to make yours stand out from the crowd!

DISCURSIVE WRITING

> 7.   Many pupils in Scotland have to wear school uniform to school. Give your views.
>
> 15. The Scottish Government has banned smoking in public places such as restaurants. Give your views.
>
> 16. Watching too much television is bad for you. Give your views.

This type of writing should not be attempted unless you have thought about the subject before the exam! If you have never reflected on the smoking ban and don't really care if people smoke or not, you are not going to write a convincing essay.

You should try to include facts and information in Discursive Writing and you will only have these if you have read or thought about the topic in advance. For example, if you are writing about school uniform, do you know how many pupils in Scotland wear school uniform, or have information about the benefits of wearing uniform? Background knowledge always improves Discursive Writing because it shows you are knowledgeable about the topic and have already thought about it.

If you choose to write a Discursive essay, you should be very organised as organisation is a very important aspect of this type of writing!

The first thing to do is to decide what you think about the topic. Do you agree, disagree or can you understand both sides of the argument? You should state your opinion about this clearly at the beginning of your essay. This will be your introductory paragraph.

You will then explain the arguments for or against (or both) in the main body of the essay. The way to organise this clearly is to use topic sentences. The topic sentence is usually the first sentence in a paragraph although it can actually occur anywhere in the paragraph. (Why not try experimenting with writing a paragraph and placing the topic sentences in different places within the paragraph?) The topic sentence explains the main point you make in the paragraph, for example, you think zoos are cruel because all the animals are caged or locked in. Remember that you should include information and examples in each paragraph too.

Your conclusion should repeat your opinion clearly and finish off your essay strongly.

TOP TIP

It's important to stick to your opinion – don't change your mind halfway through! You either agree, disagree or you can understand both sides. Make sure the end of your essay matches the beginning!

CREDIT CRUNCH

To improve on your discursive writing skills – and hopefully be awarded a top grade – ensure that your ideas are complex and that you organise your ideas and arguments very clearly.

You also need to:

- be objective; in other words, show you can 'stand back' from the topic, for example, by showing understanding of others' opinions
- generalise; in other words, show you can make general statements as well as using specific examples
- evaluate; in other words, show you can make a judgement about your own and others' points of view

Have a look at *Standard Grade English Course Notes* for lots more advice about Discursive Writing.

WRITING IN A SPECIFIC FORMAT

3. Write a letter of complaint to a travel company about poor holiday accommodation.

11. Write an article for your school newspaper or magazine about any aspect of the environment, for example, global warming or pollution.

Question 3 asks you to write a letter. If you choose this question, you must be familiar with the correct layout for a letter.

Can you remember all the rules about the layout and language in this type of letter?

- Where should you write your address?
- Where should you add the date?
- Should you include the address you are writing to?
- How should you start your letter?
- What do you call the person you are writing to?
- Should you use paragraphs?
- How do you finish off the letter?

If you are unclear about how to set out letters, don't try this question!

Letters also need to have a clear structure – look at the suggested structure below for a letter of complaint.

Introduction – state clearly the issue you wish to write/complain about.

        Explain your opinion about it.

        Give some facts and figures which support your opinion.

Middle section – explain in more detail about the problem.

        Give examples of what this means/has meant for you/your community.

Conclusion – restate your opinion.

        Explain what you want to be done about the situation. For example, you could make positive suggestions about alternatives.

Question 11 asks you to write an article. If you choose this question, you must be familiar with writing this kind of article – the language you use must be suitable and you should organise your writing carefully. This article is for a school newspaper or magazine so would the audience be pupils, parents, teachers or others? The article must be written in an appropriate way depending on who will read it.

Articles usually make clear what the article is about in the first paragraph – this is a summary of the issue. Then you might decide on a number of paragraphs, for example:

1. Introductory paragraph
2. What is global warming?
3. Dangers of global warming
4. Reasons for global warming
5. Solutions
6. What the school can do to stop global warming
7. Why school action is so important

There are occasionally questions which ask you to write in other formats, for example, a speech or a diary or a play script. There is not enough space here to advise on all these types. However, you should attempt this type of question only if you are very familiar with the format, layout and language you should use.

DESCRIPTIVE WRITING

19. Describe the scene brought to mind by one of the following:

    'I look at the night
    and make nothing of it –
    those black pages
    with no print.'
    OR
    'So many summers and I have lived them too.'

This is one of the most challenging types of writing – but if you are a confident writer with a very well developed vocabulary, it could be the one for you!

- Do you love using imagery and description, and can you use plenty of adjectives in original ways?
- Are you able to describe a person, an object, a landscape for longer than a few paragraphs?
- Are you able to organise your descriptive writing? For example, you might decide to describe each aspect of the scene in turn and so you will have to work out an order for this.

TOP TIP

Don't forget to appeal to all five senses in descriptive writing – not just what you can see in the scene.

- What can be heard?
- What can be touched or felt? What textures are there?
- What can be smelled?
- What can be tasted?

If you enjoy Descriptive Writing, it can be tempting just to write randomly all sorts of great descriptive words and phrases as they come to you! But a descriptive essay needs to have some kind of logical order so that the reader can follow it clearly.

Could you:

- use the five senses as five 'sections' in your essay?
- describe each aspect of the scene in turn, for example, night, darkness, trees?
- describe the scene from different places, as though you are moving through the scene, for example, the darkness from ground level, halfway up a hill, at the top of the hill?

> **TOP TIP**
>
> To improve your descriptive writing, look at photographs or pictures and practise describing these in as much detail as you can.
>
> Remember that you have 75 minutes to write in the exam so you need to include as much detail as possible!

WRITE IN ANY WAY

4. Write in any way you like about the picture.
8. 'Too Cool for School'. Write in any way you like using this title.
12. Write in any way you like about the picture.
17. 'We All Make Mistakes'. Write in any way you like about this title.
18. Bill Shankly, a famous football club manager, once said 'Some people think football is a matter of life and death. I assure you it's much more serious than that.' Write in any way you like about football or any other sport.

These questions are great if you do not find a question in the paper which springs out at you – or if you are good at lots of types of writing. These questions give you freedom to choose what genre you want to write. You could write a poem, a drama script, a fictional diary … just remember that you have to be confident and experienced in writing the genre you choose.

Of course, all the usual rules apply – planning your writing, organising it well with a clear structure, expressing yourself clearly and well – whatever you write!

> **CREDIT CRUNCH**
>
> Whichever type of writing you choose in the exam, for a Credit grade, your ideas and/or information has to be well organised. On top of that, try to demonstrate to the examiner that you can 'select and highlight' what is most significant. Linking words and phrases can help with this, as can thinking about the order of your ideas.